Puzzling Portmeirion
An Unconventional Guide to a Curious Destination

Copyright © 2007 by Craig Conley. All rights reserved.

Table of Contents

In Search of a Gold Leaf Shadow 5
Portmeirion as Virtual Reality 7
Locating Temporal Vortices 15
Locating Spatial Anomalies 27
How to Look at a *Trompe l'oeil* Window 30
The Shadowy, Upside Down World of the Camera Obscura 35
Quest for the Legendary Stag of Portmeirion 38
On the Tail of a Spectre-Dog 47
Gateways to the Spirit World 53
Subtle Hauntings 63
Fairies Underfoot 64
A Portrait of the Artist As Portmeirion 72
Portmeirion as a House of Tarot Cards 77
Scavenger Hunt: Golden Buddha's Missing Arm 91
Scavenger Hunt: The Architect's Signature 94
Scavenger Hunt: On the Tails of the Wild Sea-Fairies 96
Scavenger Hunt: The Elusive Unicorn 101
Scavenger Hunt: Grotesqueries 103
Scavenger Hunt: Mother and Cherub Reunion 106
Scavenger Hunt: Bells and Whistles 109
Scavenger Hunt: Paragons of Virtue 114
Portmeirion as a Sailor's Knot 120
Woodland Trail Maps 121

In Search of a Gold Leaf Shadow

Oft Upon a Time

Every fairy tale has a twilit undercurrent, but Sir Clough Williams-Ellis' fantastical village of Portmeirion casts a shadow of gold. Recall the fairy tale of Jack Horner, concerning a knight from a "vastly ancient and noble family" whose members had the exclusive honor of "being born with shadows of gold-leaf attached to them instead of the vulgar grey and sometimes black shadows that adhere to common people."[1] Clough was certainly a godson to that knight, for the brighter the sunlight, the brighter his architectural silhouette. Like a modern Phantasmion, Clough traced the outline of his radiant shadow to create a seemingly substantial village of "redoubled brightness" and "many-colored radiance."[2] There are no secret skeletons tucked away in dark closets at Portmeirion—every embarrassment of riches is proudly on display, and every cloister is not only doorless but open on both sides. Still, shadow hunters must tread carefully, for delicate gold-leaf tears easily. Indeed, fragility reflects off every gaily painted stone and whimsical adornment in the village. Hidden in plain view, fragility is the true secret of Portmeirion's exquisite charm.

A golden Burmese dancer balances atop an Ionic pillar in Portmeirion's piazza. Telford's Tower rises in the background.

---

1   S. Baring Gould, *The Crock of Gold: Twelve Fairy Tales, Old and New* (1899)
2   Sara Coleridge, *Phantasmion: A Fairy Tale* (1874)

Portmeirion weaves its story from wispy threads gathered all across Europe, layering themes upon themes into a billowing tapestry where everything old is new again. Each building rose from secondhand rubble, antiquated bricks and ornaments repurposed and reborn to tell an alternate history—a future history, even. "The true fairy-tale poet is a seer into the hereafter," suggested Novalis (c. 1799). "The genuine fairy tale must be prophetic description—idealistic description."[3] Clough was a one-of-a-kind prophesying poet, his imagery so vivid as to invite pilgrims to step inside and experience eternity firsthand.

In this unconventional guidebook we will explore Clough's trailblazing experiments in virtual reality, his subtle but powerful time-warping and space-folding tricks, the little-known myths and legends echoing down every footpath, and the myriad restless spirits at play. Eccentric globe-trotters will have their eyes opened, curiosities piqued, intellects tickled, feet motivated, and pens recording the most fascinating entries in their travel diaries, bar none.

A view of the village from the Camera Obscura.

---

3   qtd. in David Frederick Haight and Marjorie A. Haight, *Scandal of Reason* (2004)

Portmeirion as Virtual Reality

A Surreal Mindscape

> A charming place, but unreal, like a picture postcard brought to life.
> —Cecily Mackworth, *Ends of the World* (1987)

Virtual reality for the masses? It's already here, and you don't need a high-tech headset, goggles, or gloves. It's at Portmeirion, where reality and illusion are indistinguishable. But don't be fooled by glossy brochures: Portmeirion is no candy-colored utopian community. It's more like an elaborate contraption from a bizarre science fiction novel, manipulating its visitors in undreamt-of ways. As with a video game, if you have a grasp of how things operate, you can play along and increase your level of fun.

Portmeirion opened to the public in 1926 (nearly 30 years before Disneyland) and was experimenting with virtual reality decades before the term was coined. Columnist Nicholas De Jongh writes that "to see the place is like traveling into someone else's vision."[1] Portmeirion was "built by someone who never left childhood completely. It's a world which the subconscious would know and recognize as invented rather than seen."

The mother of all themed environments sends you tumbling mind, body, and spirit into the heart of invention. Consider:

- You find yourself standing in front of a town hall, yet this is a village with no residents, only guests.

A town hall serving no citizenry.

---

1   "The Dreamer Architect," *Crawdaddy* (May 1978)

The village as seen from the centenary Gazebo

- Phony picture windows are meant to be looked at, not looked through.

- The town square is surrounded by bright, Italianate pavilions, seemingly having gotten "lost in a storm and accidentally land[ing] on the shores of the Atlantic Ocean as opposed to their familiar Mediterranean Sea."[2]

- The buildings' vibrant colors (white, green turquoise, ochre, terracotta, yellow, orange, cobalt blue, and pink) are "thoroughly disorienting."[3]

- "Space ebbs and flows like water into small pools and dramatic, open cascades."[4] Individual buildings are in fact jumbles of salvaged materials from all over Europe.

- With the warping of space, time itself is twisted: buildings from different historical periods stand side by side, while plaques on

---

[2] Michael Zlatkovsky, "Tales of a Rambling Rover," Harlac's Tongue Blog (March 26, 2007)
[3] Patricia Brooks and Lester Brooks, *Crown Insider's Guide to Britain* (1987)
[4] Charles Jencks, *The New Paradigm in Architecture: The Language of Postmodernism* (2002)

statues memorialize not single years but multiple centuries at once.

- "On a clear day . . . one is captured in a 360 degree sensurround screen of architectural fantasy, sea, sunshine, sand and, occasionally, snow on the surrounding peaks."[5]

Various time streams converge at the Hercules pedestal. Plaques celebrate several different years.

- It's a port, yet the estuary is so shallow that only the occasional dinghy can approach.

- There's a lighthouse on a rocky promontory, but no light.

- There's a boat on the harbor, but it's permanently anchored because it is in fact a *building* made of stone (complete with slate floor), serving as a retaining wall.

The Amis Reunis is a boat-shaped retaining wall below the main hotel building.

[5] Katy Chance, "Portmeirion" Chance.co.za (2007)

People can't even agree on how "substantial" the village is. Travel critic Jan Morris calls it "a floating fantasy above the sea . . . the whole thing . . . clustered with an airy flimsiness on its steep slope, as though one day it might slide all on top of itself into the water."[6] In direct contradiction, *Country Life* says that "At Portmeirion the buildings almost literally grew out of the rock and were intended to look as if they did."[7]

Ramshackle or sturdy? Exotic or traditional? Practical or whimsical? Cluttered or immaculate? The virtual reality of Portmeirion defies easy categorization. In this topsy-turvy world, petrol pumps are ornaments, gilded Burmese dancers stand atop Ionic columns, and a giant Buddha sits under a pantiled loggia. "Portmeirion is in turns foreign and then strangely familiar, beautiful but not in an ordinary kind of way."[8] Around every corner, Clough's magic wand manipulates our perceptions to create a wholly artificial reality. The remarkable thing is that most of the tricks are subliminal. Architectural sleights such as forced perspective and gradiented paint make buildings seem taller—or smaller—than they really are. For instance, the height of the Campanile has been so exaggerated that the top is actually only one-half size. The walls of the Gate House cottage feature three different shades

A "forced perspective" architectural technique makes buildings such as the Campanile and Bridge House seem taller.

---

6   *The Matter of Wales* (1984)
7   Sept. 16, 1976
8   Ricki Crookes, "Portmeirion," UK-Holidays.com (2007)

of paint, lightest at the top and darkest below. Oversized chimneys, extremely low arches, reduced upper stories, and small statues also create illusions of height and distance.[9] Such manipulation makes a building more welcoming and accessible. According to Clough, "Portmeirion is . . . very definitely scaled down, and if not strictly 'miniature' is none the less rather cozily compact and intimate."

Who could keep track of Portmeirion's total control of your environment? In designing his village, Clough avoided symmetry in order to achieve movement, deliberately accenting a sudden elevation in landscape, for example, so that your eye is forced to keep moving up. Everywhere you look, views are deliberately framed by archways, doorways, and sculpted vegetation.

Scaled down architecture lends an air of intimacy.

Views are deliberately framed by archways.

However, lest visitors wander about like puppets, expectations are dashed at every opportunity—buildings with towers or battlements aren't fortresses, for example, nor do pinnacles or flying buttresses signify a church. Stately columns may not support much of anything, and ornate doorways likely lead to nowhere. The entire village is "rich in the unexpected: odd angles, surprising little balconies, curious juxtapositions."[10] The grand design is meant to be a feast for

---

9   John Cornforth, "Portmeirion Revisited," *Country Life* (Sept. 16, 1976)
10 Christopher Hussey, *The Picturesque: Studies in a Point of View* (1967)

the mind as well as the eyes. The visitor is meant to think outside the box, to get lost in another dimension, to stumble upon spontaneous drama, to fire forgotten synapses hidden in the recesses of the brain, to discover the missing pieces of a seemingly finished puzzle.

Interestingly, the follies of Portmeirion are boldly presented, without apology. The *trompe l'oeils* at every turn are effective, but don't fool so much as intrigue. Clough not only produces illusion but—in confessing it—stimulates the desire for it. A real threshold can be found in any building, and as a rule it will lead to somewhere unextraordinary, but Portmeirion tells us that folly thresholds correspond "much more to our daydream demands."[11]

This mermaid statue is actually a painting on sheet metal—an illusion which invites close inspection.

Portmeirion tends to strike visitors as otherworldly, like "the site of a fabled Brigadoon."[12] But what, exactly, do we associate with the fanciful? The terraced gardens and cobbled squares are all imbued with idealism and desire. The buildings are picturesque through the *sentiment* they inspire. We unconsciously associate the campanile, for example, with romance and mystery. The virtual reality tugs at the strings of our emotions.

---

11 Umberto Eco, *Travels in Hyperreality* (1983)
12 *Travel-Holiday* (May 1980)

A Dream World Built of Stone

> The extraordinary village of Portmeirion...
> looks as if it was conceived in a colourful dream.
> —Rebecca Ford, Footprint Wales (2005)

Years before the construction of Portmeirion, historian of technology Lewis Mumford foresaw how a dreamer architect could build a fantasy realm out of worldly materials. Later, Mumford so admired Portmeirion that he practically made it his second home. The following brief sketch of his book The Study of Utopias (1922) should help to demonstrate why he found the village so captivating, as well as to illuminate the programming behind Clough's virtual reality.

Mumford begins by suggesting that what makes human history interesting is that we live in two worlds: the one within and the one without. The world within includes all the fantasies and projections that pattern people's behavior. Mumford observes that the physical world is inescapable, but the world of ideas exists on another plane. It is our substitute for the external world—a kind of home to which we flee when reality becomes too much.

At the same time, the world within serves to sort and sift our everyday concerns, "and a new sort of reality is projected back again upon the external world," Mumford says. This serves one of two functions: as a means for escape or compensation that releases us from our daily frustrations, or as a means for providing "a condition for our release in the future." The second function seeks to change the external world so that one can deal with it on one's own terms. Mumford explains that in the first function, "we build impossible castles in the air," while in the other we hire an architect and a mason and begin to build an environment which meets our essential needs.

Utopias of escape are good only for short visits, however, because they are imaginary. Perfection would be unstimulating and paralyzing. But "Utopias of reconstruction" seek to alter the physical world and the mental framework of the people who live there. Mumford notes that we can't dismiss our ideals from the facts of our lives. "[T]he things we dream of tend consciously or unconsciously to work themselves out in the pattern of our daily lives," he writes. "We need not abandon the real world in order to enter these realizable worlds; for it is out of the first that the second are always coming."

So Mumford must have found in Portmeirion's reconstructed buildings a testimonial to his belief that humankind can realize its Utopian dreams in the physical world. Indeed, Clough stated frequently that his ideal was to develop a beautiful location without spoiling it, and even to enhance its natural beauties. His finished product proved to be more than a mere fanciful extravagance (as his critics would have it). Portmeirion remains today a good commercial business. For all its visitors, the village is a "no-place" where we can actually spend the night and forget the ugly problems of the "real world" outside. And this virtual reality might even inspire us to dream up some of our own plans.

I picked up a pinky-size fragment of stucco painted turquoise from a housekeeper's pile of sweepings of palm fronds and pebbles.... I keep the artifact next to my computer, in case I am ever tempted to think that my trip to Portmeirion was a dream.
—Eve M. Kahn, "A Man's Whim on the Welsh Coast," *The New York Times* (July 29, 2007)

Locating Temporal Vortices

> I was warped in the folds of time, like a reflection in a fun house mirror.
> —Haruki Marakammi, *Dance Dance Dance* (1994)

The Spiraling March of Time

Like a needle piercing the fabric of space/time, a monument typically establishes and "fixes" an historical moment. For example, the lion statue behind the Gothic Pavilion is inscribed to freeze in time one special birthday celebration in 1973:

> Presented to Portmeirion and its Founder, Sir Clough Williams-Ellis, by his friends and colleagues on his 90th birthday, May 28th 1973.

The lion statue behind the Gothic Pavilion

However, other Portmeirion monuments diabolically serve a diametric purpose: to spin the river of time into a dizzying whirlpool! Let's consider some examples of plaques on statues and structures that serve as dials rather than pinpoints.

Hercules Does a Pirouette

First stop is William Brodie's Hercules statue (cast c. 1863), erected in front of Hercules Hall and at the top of the Hercules Steps. Attached to the base of the statue are several engraved tablets:

• To the summer of 1959, in honour of its splendour

The Hercules statue by Hercules Hall

- 1971 Highly Commended
- 1975 excelled even 1959
- Nonesuch 1976

Instead of commemorating a single splendid year, like a thumbtack on a calendar, these multiple plaques send the march of time into a maelstrom. Better, let's imagine time as a river; the years flow around and around the Hercules statue like a whirlpool around a boulder.

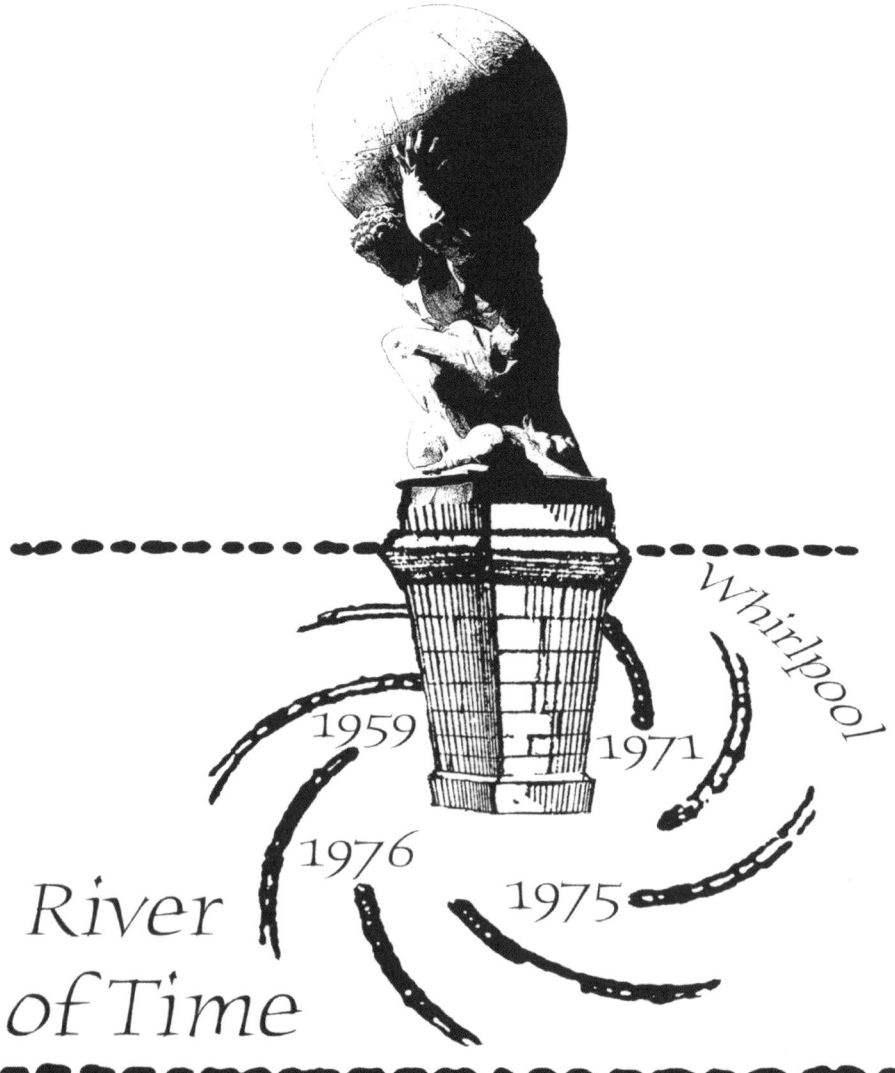

The years flow around the Hercules statue.

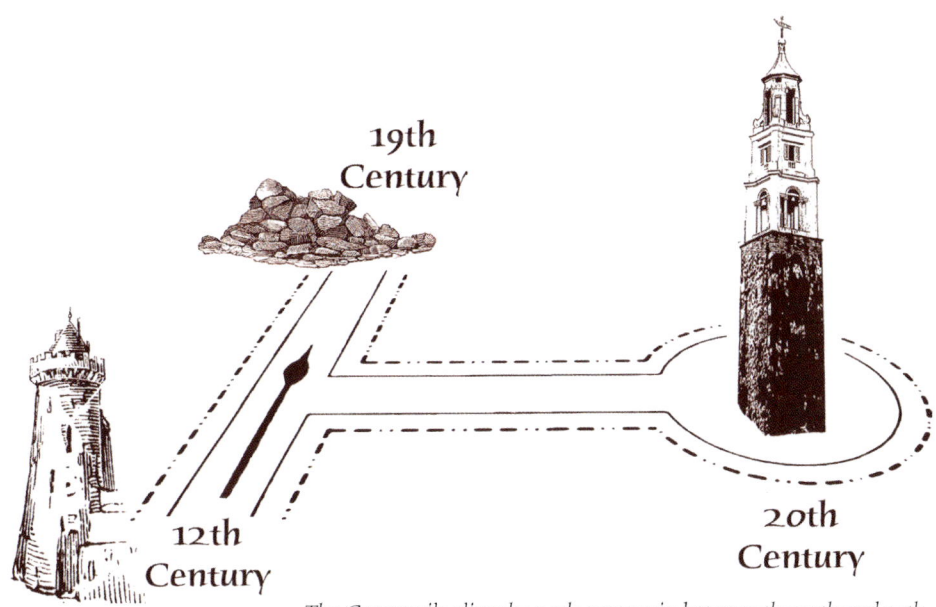

The Campanile slips the 20th century in between the 12th and 19th.

The Bell Tower: Chiming the Centuries

Next stop, the Campanile (constructed 1928). It should be noted that this area is accessible only by overnight guests of the village, so if you're a day visitor, consider staying the evening. The plaque at the base of the tower bears the following inscription:

> This tower, built in 1928 by Clough Williams-Ellis, architect and publican, embodies stones from the 12th century castle of his ancestor Gruffydd ap Cynan, King of North Wales, that stood on an eminence 150 yards to the west. It was finally razed c. 1869 by Sir William Fothergill Cook, inventor of the Electric Telegraph, "lest the ruins should become known and attract visitors to the place." This 19th century affront to the 12th is thus piously redressed in the 20th.

Unlike at the Hercules statue, this is a single plaque, but it encompasses no fewer than eight centuries. Interestingly, Clough makes a knot of the timestream, slipping the 20th century in between the 12th and

19th. In his dedication, he actually has the reader counting the centuries backward and forward, thusly: 19, 12, 20. The flow of time is effectively warped. Clough's "redress" is also a regress, just as the "affront" takes us aback.

The Bell Tower as the Reflection of a Platonic Ideal

The Campanile plaque invites another intriguing perspective, involving the theory of Platonic idealism. According to Plato's view, our changeable material world is merely an imperfect reflection of a higher, unchanging principle. So the perfect ideal castle transcends its material creation and destruction throughout the centuries. Following Plato's philosophy, the ideal castle inspired the 12th century construction of Castell Deudraeth, was impervious to the 19th century razing, and bolstered Clough's 20th century reparation in the form of the Portmeirion bell tower.

A folly ruined fort in honor of the 12th century Castell Deudraeth, near the centenary Gazebo.

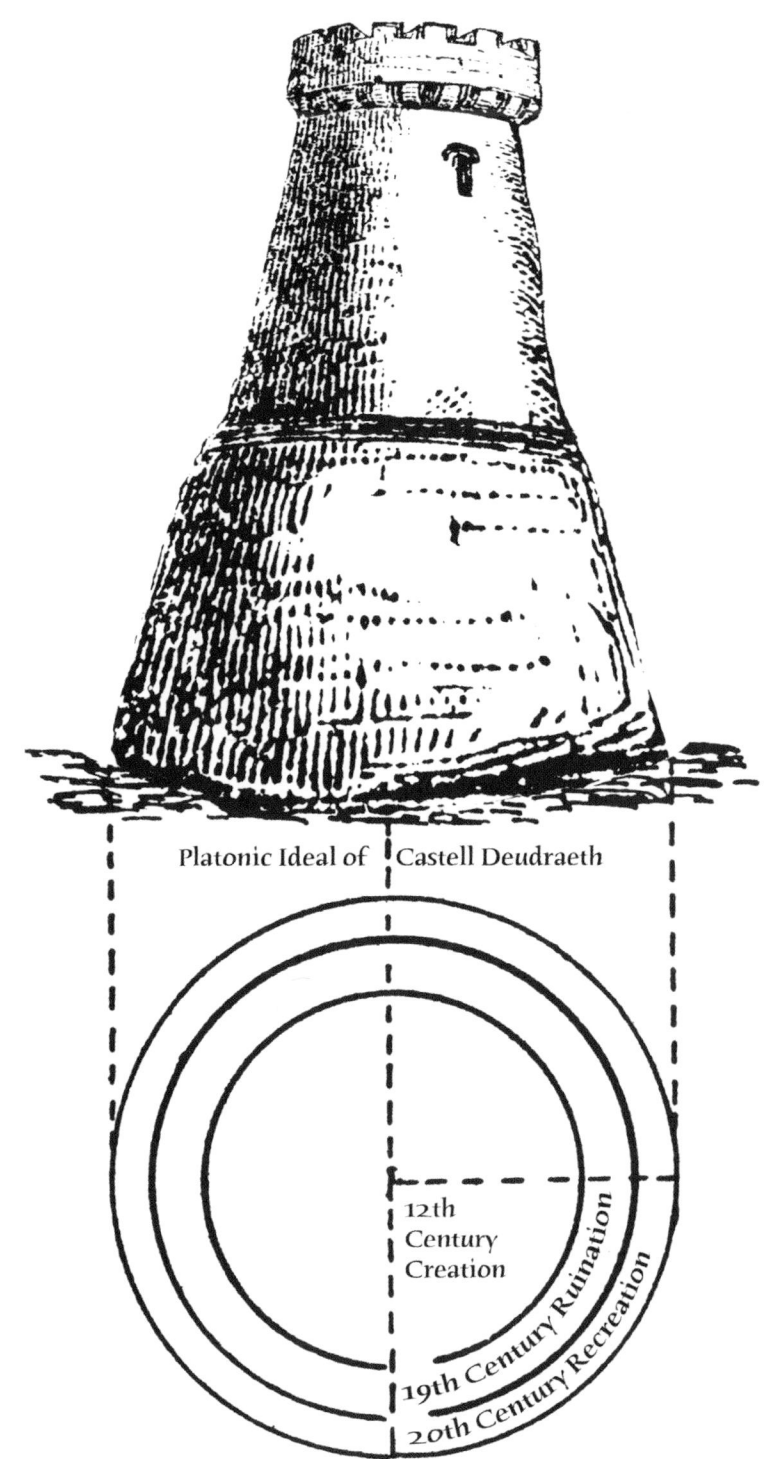

Platonic Ideal of Castell Deudraeth

12th Century Creation
19th Century Ruination
20th Century Recreation

Concurrent Architectural Periods

Though Italianate in feel, the wildly different buildings that comprise Portmeirion represent an array of architectural periods, seamlessly merged. Following are just a few examples of periods and styles, primarily gathered by Portmeirion expert Marsha McCurley:

Palladian/Georgian:	Cliff House, Unicorn
Rococo:	Triumphal Arch
Georgian:	Belvedere
Baroque:	Round House, Facade doorway into Prior's Lodging, Top of Campanile
James Pryde windows:	Prior's Lodging, Chantry
Romanesque:	Base of Campanile
Jacobean:	Hercules Hall
Gothic:	Bristol Colonnade, Gothic Pavilion
Victorian Gothic:	Castell Deudraeth
Renaissance Gothic:	Front of Pantheon
Dutch:	Salutation

Hence, any casual walk through the winding streets of the village entails time travel. But look more closely. Like a fractal, individual structures reflect multiple styles as well. With bits and pieces gathered from all over Europe, these salvaged buildings hold memories of earlier eras.[1] Following are some prime examples:

- The Pantheon (*Y Gromen*) features an ornate façade which Clough salvaged from the demolition of the Ismay home (c. 1882) in

---

1 William John Mitchell, *The Poetics of Gardens* (1993)

Dawpool, Cheshire, where it served as a fireplace surround. The High Cloister, as it was known, stood in situ for 20 years before the dome was constructed behind it.

- The Campanile (*Y Twr Clychau*) was constructed using stones recovered from a ruined 12th century castle. The turret clock which adorns the tower's belfry hails from an early 19th century London brewery.

The Pantheon

- The Gloriette (*Yr Orchestfa*) consists of four Ionic columns rescued from Hooton Hall in Cheshire. Clough acquired eight columns from its 18th century Colonnade. They lay idle on the grounds at Portmeirion for over 30 years until the Gloriette's conception, when they were found buried beneath a garden which had developed on top of them.

- The Gothic Pavilion (*Pafiliwn Gothig*) is a careful reassembly of materials obtained from the slipshod demolition of a Gothic porch which had been added to Nercwys Hall in Flintshire during the early 19th century.

- The Amis Reunis, or Stone Boat, is a careful reconstruction of a trading ketch which Clough kept moored in the same spot on the quay. The ship aground consists largely of

The Gothic Pavilion

materials salvaged from the original ship, which had been nearly destroyed during a sudden gale.

- The centerpiece of Bridge House (*Ty Pont*) is its diamond-paned Venetian window which Clough obtained from Arnos Court with the Bristol Colonnade.

- Battery (*Y Batri*) is so-named by virtue of the cannons which keep watch over the estuary from its cliffside terrace (accessible by overnight guests). Clough acquired the cannons from Belan Fort near Caernarfon, which had been built by Thomas Wynn (Lord Newborough, c. 1775) to fortify the Menai Straits during the Napoleonic wars.

- The Bristol Colonnade (*Colofnres Bryste*) was erected in Bristol at Arnos Court during the late 18th century as a resplendent façade to its bathhouse. Damaged by bombs, the structure's

The Venetian window of the Bridge House.

The Bristol Colonnade, facing the Piazza.

arduous relocation to Portmeirion involved the precise numbering of each stone prior to disassembly.

- Hercules Hall (*Neuadd Ercwlff*) is a majestic structure designed around a central ballroom crowned by a captivating Jacobean ceiling which had been installed at Emral Hall in Flintshire in the early 17th century. Clough acquired the ceiling, which depicts the labors of Hercules, at auction prior to the demolition of Emral. Hercules Hall features numerous elements from Emral, as well as a grille salvaged from the Old Bank of England.

Hercules Hall

Photographing Portmeirion On Its Own Terms

In August 2006, photographer Gareth Courage experimented with some time twisting of his own, loading his Kodak Cresta with Ilford film that had expired in the autumn of 1965. He described the film as being "as expired as film gets without vanishing." What better way to photograph Portmeirion than with an old camera and long-expired film? The result is reminiscent of 19th century copper plate printing. The images seem to reveal, in the words of one commentator, a signal hidden underneath the noise of strange static.

The Bristol Colonnade and Chantry cottage through the fog of long-expired film. Photo by Gareth Courage.

Above, the modern-day Pantheon is eerily captured on long-expired film. Below, Chantry cottage rises atop a hill. Photos by Gareth Courage.

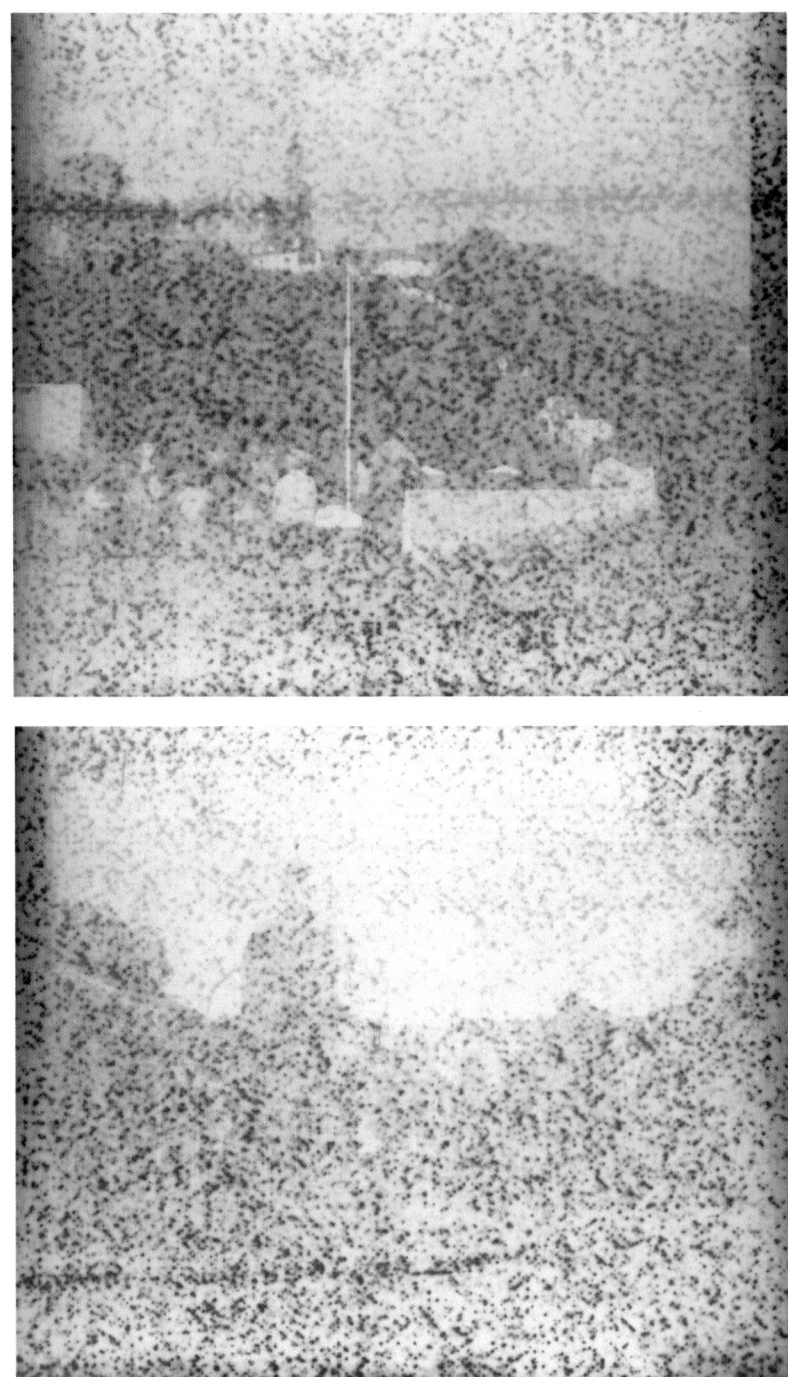

Above, the village rises above the estuary, on long-expired film.
Below, the skyline from the piazza. Photos by Gareth Courage.

Locating Spatial Anomalies

Stretching Space

Just as Portmeirion warps time, it stretches space. A journey through the picturesque village seems twice as long as an equal-length walk through a city. Such is the surprising finding of the Manchester University School of Environment and Development, which tested pedestrians in Portmeirion in 2006. Before we explore the results of that test, make your own estimate of the following route, from the arched entrance to the dock at the lighthouse. How many miles is it?

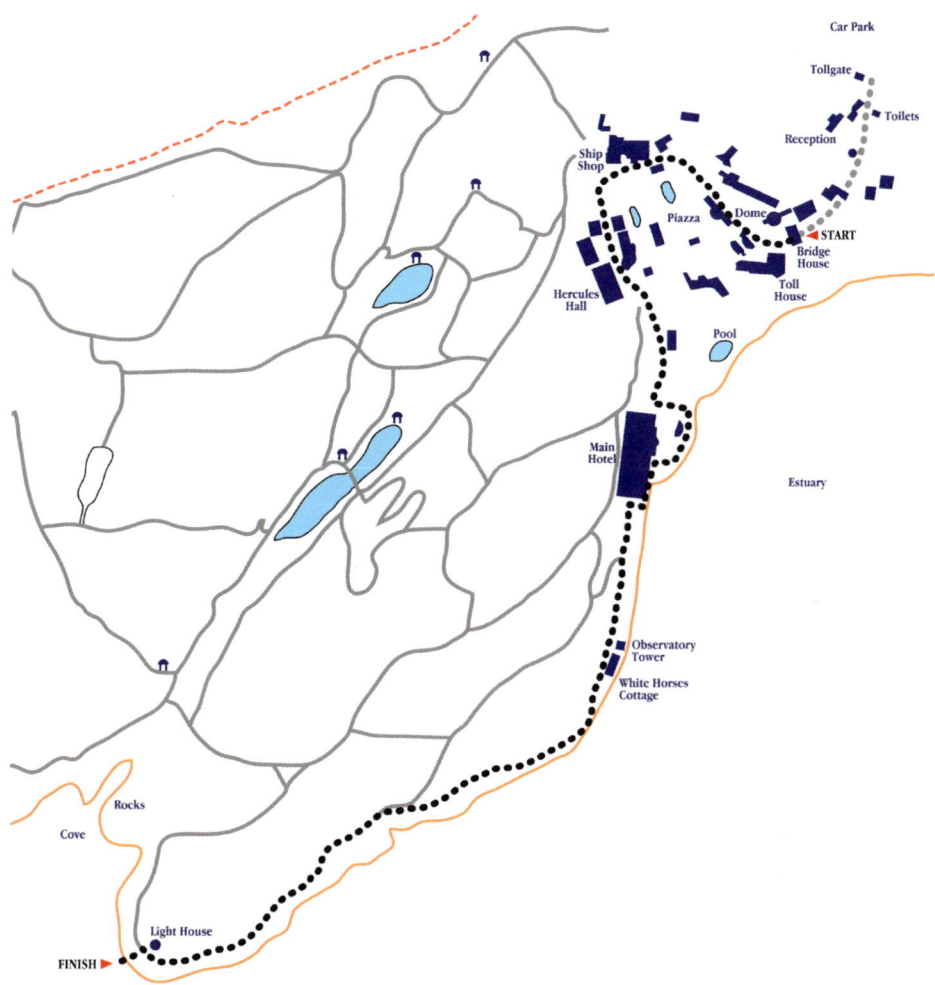

Researchers Andrew Crompton and Frank Brown compared estimates of first year architecture students walking 500 meters down a straight road in the city of Manchester with estimates of a route of the same distance in Portmeirion. Estimates at Portmeirion were, on average, double those of the same distance in Manchester.

Portmeirion's secret? Cues in the environment influence our perception of space, and Portmeirion "fulfills all the known requirements for appearing large."[1] Whereas pedestrians in Manchester walk purposefully, with their eyes forward or down, tourists at Portmeirion wander around looking every which way. "The more turns, slopes, intersections, and features a walk has, the longer it appears. . . . [T]he more information there is to be observed about a journey, the longer it will seem."[2]

One of the ways we orient ourselves to an urban space is judging the distances of objects in plain view. Researchers have shown that the human visual system has evolved to make reasonable statistical guesses about distances within a visual scene. When our expectations are upset, however, we become susceptible to "illusions of perception." One way Portmeirion upsets expectations is through scale. Crompton and Brown explain that the village

> is built to a smaller than normal scale, with many little places to pause and sit or to look at the view. Most of its buildings are reputed to be approximately seven-eighths normal size. . . . Parts of old buildings have been imported and recycled in unusual ways, giving an appearance of picturesque sham antiquity. On high ground, a romantic tower and domed building seem imposing from below but become rather small when approached. There is no traffic in the narrow lanes. Buildings are laid out informally in a garden setting surrounded by mature woodland dotted with follies, with paths and vista connecting places in unexpected ways. Throughout the village, outcrops of finely fissured slate give a peculiar impression of

---

[1] Andrew Crompton and Frank Brown, "Distance Estimation in a Small-Scale Environment," *Environment and Behavior* 2006;38;656
[2] Ibid.

being miniaturized. Portmeirion has a mix of differently sized spaces, from the intimate to the huge open space of the bay across which distant hills are visible. This complexity makes it a good place to play hide-and-seek. . . . The lack of familiar street furniture, signs, or other objects in common with more ordinary places deprives the visitor of references for scale and contributes to Portmeirion's otherworldly atmosphere.[3]

The actual distance to be estimated in the study was 0.31 miles. The average estimate in Manchester was one-half mile. The average estimate in Portmeirion was 0.93 miles—three times the actual distance. All but one of the 69 Portmeirion participants overestimated the distance.[4]

Interestingly, travel time is not a factor in distance perception. Walking through an area slowly doesn't make it seem bigger. However, distances do seem to increase if the number of turns and intersections goes up. Similarly, "boundary height, ground texture, and the presence of isolated elements" are factors that enlarge one's subjective perception of an environment. The more interesting and complicated an area, the more "places to stop, sit and look," and "all the things that give Portmeirion its charm and human scale will therefore make it seem larger than places where one keeps moving, where there are few places to linger, and scale is determined by cars."[5]

Unicorn Cottage appears to be a grand two-story building but in fact has only one floor.

---

3   Ibid.
4   Ibid.
5   Ibid.

How to Look at a *Trompe l'oeil* Window

Superflat Art

"Superflat" is a concept coined by the contemporary artist Takashi Murakami, whose paintings present a depthless two-dimensional space "devoid of perspective and devoid of hierarchy, all existing equally and simultaneously."[1] Steep terrain aside, one could view Portmeirion as a superflat creation, where perspectives are deliberately distorted, different architectural styles exist side by side, and salvaged junk is showcased as high art. Murakami's approach, which traces back to "traditional Japanese techniques pioneered by the panel and screen painters of the sixteenth century," is intended to make one smile, to broaden one's horizons, and to challenge one's percep-

A trompe l'oeil window near the tollgate, painted onto the face of a wall.

---

1 *BT Monthly Art Magazine*, Japan, Issue 5, May 2000, qtd. by Nick Curry, "Thought for the Day: Superflat," Imomus.com/thought280600.html

tions of what constitutes high art.[2] Clough's intent was identical. In a superflat world, where the exalted and the lowly are equalized, we experience that transcendent "ah-ha" moment—what the mythologist Joseph Campbell called "aesthetic arrest"—not in a shrine or a museum, but around every corner. To recontextualize art critic Nick Curry[3], Portmeirion's superflat *trompe l'oeils* bring enchantment to the banal activity of window shopping, for we're invited to look *at* the painted windows, not through them.

Fake Windows Everywhere

Let's go window shopping, superflat Portmeirion style. How many *trompe l'oeil* windows can you spot? Here's a list of places to check:

- Cliff House sports seven windows on its front, the right hand three of which are fake (complete with painted lace curtains). The six fancy windows on the side of the cottage are also fake: artist Nigel Simmons not only painted curtains but also reflections of nearby architecture.

The top right and two bottom right windows on the Cliff House are painted on.

2 Guy Hepner Contemporary, GuyHepner.com (2004)
3 Nick Curry, "Thought for the Day: Superflat," Imomus.com/thought280600.html

- The center window on the patio of the Salutation building (Ship Shop) is a mural by Susan Williams-Ellis (restored by Nigel Simmons). The painting presents the illusion of seeing all the way through the shop and out the window on the other side.

- The sheltered entrance to Fountain Cottage has a false window with a painted view of its interior.

The trompe l'oeil window at the entrance to Fountain Cottage.

- There is an elaborate false window near the tollgate, depicting a person peering through.

- The five windows surrounding the Gloriette's open doorway are fake.

- The top windows of Chantry Row are fakes, creating the illusion of a second floor.

- The top windows on the front of the Arches building are fakes.

- The two windows on the side of White Horses cottage are painted.

- A devil figure is painted in a false window at the top of the estuary side of Government House. This wall is visible to overnight guests.

Two painted windows on White Horses cottage.

A painted devil peers from a Government House window.

A trompe l'oeil window on Chantry Row, complete with painted curtains.

An entire side of Cliff House is painted on.

The Shadowy, Upside Down World of the Camera Obscura

The Eye of God On the Universe

> The complement of light is shadow....
> Shadow is the latent vehicle of a device called the
> camera obscura.
> —Lyn Pocock & Judson Rosebush, *The Computer
> Animator's Technical Handbook* (2001)

Divine. Incomparable. Rapturous. Charming. Ecstatic. Delightful. Beholders of the camera obscura (literally "dark room" in Latin) have used such enthusiastic words[1] to describe a unique experience of "inimitable beauty"[2] and brilliance projected within a shadowy chamber. Discovered by Aristotle, the camera obscura was popularized in the mid-16th century by the Italian wizard and scientist Giovanni Battista Della Porta. Considered magical and even associated with the occult arts, cameras obscura were historically "off-limits to commoners."[3] Why? Like magic lanterns, these optical oddities amuse,

The Camera Obscura alongside the estuary.

---

1   Marcus Aurelius Root, *The Camera and the Pencil* (1864)
2   Hugh Honour, *A World History of Art* (2005)
3   Robert E. Krebbs, *Groundbreaking Scientific Experiments, Inventions, and Discoveries of the Middle Ages and the Renaissance* (2004)

surprise, and mystify with transient "fairy images."[4] Like a "giant eyeball," the camera obscura offers a mesmerizing alternate way of "seeing without being seen" as life moves by in "hypnotic silence."[5] The camera obscura operates as "an eye without a point of view, the eye of God on the universe," functioning to "filter psychic materials to 'attract the eye of consciousness.'"[6]

The Secret to Its Mysterious Workings

> His mind itself became a camera obscura.
> —Harry Levin, *The Power of Blackness:
> Hawthorne, Poe, Melville* (1958)

Clough designed his own camera obscura in 1935 and christened it The Observatory Tower. It rises like a lighthouse alongside the estuary, past the main hotel building, next to the White Horses cottage. The secret to its mysterious workings? Not the golden star surmounting it, but a convex lens salvaged from a German U-boat's periscope, positioned near a small light portal at the top of the tower, with a smooth white

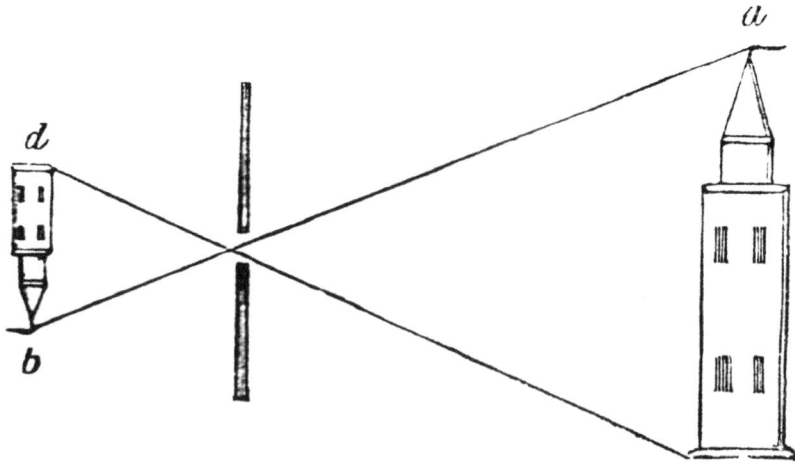

Light travels from point a along a straight path through the lens of the camera obscura to point b on the projection surface, and similarly for all points of light reflected from the object. As shown, the object thus appears inverted (mirrored and upside-down) on the projection surface.

---

4   W.J.T. Mitchell, "Benjamin and the Political Economy of the Photograph," *The Photography Reader* (2003)
5   Joseph A. Citro and Diane E. Foulds, *Curious New England: The Unconventional Traveler's Guide to Eccentric Destinations* (2003)
6   Amelia Jones, "Camera Obscura Collective," *Feminism and Visual Culture Reader* (2003)

table below to receive the upside down and backward projection. Visitors can walk inside this giant pin-hole camera and rotate the lens to enjoy a panoramic view of the village as it rises above the coastline. For an unforgettable experience, arrange to visit the Observatory Tower during an eclipse. Indeed, 10th century Muslim astronomers used cameras obscura for safely witnessing solar eclipses.[7]

Uncanny Light

> It's quite amazing, the view.
> —Ira Rankin, *Set in Darkness* (2001)

This first-hand account beautifully describes how the enormous optical apparatus uncannily sheds new light on the outside world:

> Go up into the little tower containing the camera obscura at Portmeirion, stare at the pale round table in the pitchy room, and you will see a miniature moving picture of all that you have left outside. ... [T]he people and objects in the picture are so curiously diminished and so strangely lifted from their actual surroundings into the picture rectangle they take on a significance which they do not have when seen normally by the naked eye.[8]

Clough himself perfectly summarized the enduring mystique of his camera obscura:

> There is still, to me, an abiding magic in being able to command at will the whole surrounding landscape to display itself in successive images in sharp detail and vivid colour on the white table before me.[9]

Portmeirion's Observatory Tower is off-limits to day visitors, but it is accessible by overnight guests. Requests for entrance may be made at Reception.

---

7 Robert E. Krebbs, *Groundbreaking Scientific Experiments, Inventions, and Discoveries of the Middle Ages and the Renaissance* (2004)
8 Stephen Herbert, *A History of Pre-Cinema* (2000)
9 Clough Williams-Ellis, *Portmeirion: The Place and Its Meaning* (1963)

Quest for the Legendary Stag of Portmeirion

A Mystifying Appearance and Vanishing

Mysteriously appearing[1] in the mid-1920's, a fine old stag made his home in the dark, rambling woodlands hanging above the Portmeirion estate. As the first cottages of the village were rising among the shadows of the cliffs, it was the stag who "had pushed his tracks through the undergrowth and rediscovered to the newcomers the network of walks that time had obliterated. The stag, to the delight of the neighbouring farmers, vanished quite suddenly, and like a legendary figure was never seen again."[2]

Beaten Paths to Ethereal Realms

To the mystical-minded, it is no surprise that the stag revealed a long-lost system of woodland pathways to the caretakers of the Portmeirion estate. To follow a stag is to embark upon a symbolic adventure[3] into the sacred wilderness. In Celtic lore, deer are considered faery cattle, and the royal stag is regarded as a messenger between the worlds of spirit and matter.[4] Indeed, the Celtic horned god of the forest, Cernunnos, is symbolized by the stag with his tree-like antlers. In the folklore of Wales, the supernatural stag beguiles human beings into the ethereal realms.[5] Yet the legendary stag of Portmeirion tran-

---

1 "Gardens," Portmeirion-Village.com (2002)
2 E. Maxwell Fry, "Port Meirion," *The Architects' Journal* (June 20, 1928)
3 Raven Grimassi, *Encyclopedia of Wicca and Witchcraft* (2003)
4 Ibid.
5 Ibid.

scends local lore. As the village is a tribute to Italian seaside communities, it transplants not only the architecture of the Mediterranean but also the mythology. Hence, the stag of Portmeirion may be regarded as the sacred companion of Diana, Roman goddess of nature and the hunt.

An Invitation to the Lost Mythical Land of Aberia

The stag invites us to explore not just any ethereal realm, but the "lost mythical land of Aberia."[6] In Welsh, *Aber Ia* means "frozen estuary," and the flow of time certainly feels glacial in the wilds of the peninsula. Based upon the earliest descriptions (dating back to Gerald of Wales in 1188[7]), Aberia is an exotic paradise stretching into the sea, its gardens lush with fruit, home to an assortment of animals and aquatic birds, and untouched by human hands.

Diana, Roman goddess of the hunt.

Likelihood of the Stag's Rematerialization

Could the magnificent stag of Portmeirion's magical wilderness yet reappear? Ancient lore attests to a stag's mystical powers of renewal. The *Sancti Epiphanii ad Physiologum* of 1588, a religious text and medieval bestiary, specifies that a stag lives for 50 years but can thrice renew its lifespan. It accom-

A Portmeirion stag ornament at the Ship Shop.

---

6 "Y Gwyllt: Portmeirion Gardens," MyGarden.me.uk (2006)
7 "History," Portmeirion-Village.com (2002)

plishes this by sniffing out and devouring venomous serpents, then immediately drinking from a spring. According to this philosophy, if the mysterious stag in the Portmeirion woodlands renewed its life three times, it could frolic there at least through the year 2025.

Pointers for Spotting the Antlers

Where: The best stag watching spots in the Portmeirion woodlands are along the edges of the two ponds. "In the autumn, catch the lakes on a still sunny day and it becomes difficult to say where the water begins or ends, the reflection can be so perfect."[8] For the untrained eye, the stag is easier to make out in the water's reflection, by some accounts.

For sheltered lake viewing, consider the Stone Temple gazebo which overlooks the small Temple Pond. Two other gazebos offer ideal vantage points at the Oriental Lake: the Flora Steel Shelter is at one end (behind an ornate screen), and the Asian-style Ting Gazebo is located at the other end (above the Chinese bridge).

Also recommended is the Prince of Wales Shelter, a fanciful covered bench with a view of the forest, located just inside the woodlands near the carpark. For an expansive view, don't miss the folly ruined fort

The Flora Steel Shelter at Oriental Lake.

The Prince of Wales shelter.

---

8 "Y Gwyllt: Portmeirion Gardens," MyGarden.me.uk (2006)

The Stone Temple gazebo (above) overlooks Temple Pond (below).

constructed at the top of the hill that overlooks the children's playground.

When: The best season for spotting the legendary stag is late summer to autumn. Try to coincide your stag watching with the Roman festival for Diana, which occurred in mid-August. As Diana is also a moon goddess, nights of a full moon are recommended. However, night viewing is best done from the village proper, not from the woodlands. Venturing into the dark woods will be disorienting. The Prince of Wales Shelter, so near the carpark, is recommended for those who feel they must enter the woods after dark.

October, the rutting season, is another prime time for spotting the legendary stag and hearing his territorial roar.

How: Binoculars, telescopes, cameras, and patience are recommended. Full-grown stag tracks are round, wide, and show the hollow of the foot. Stags move regularly, their hind feet overlapping the tracks made by the fore feet. Observe the direction the tracks

The Ting gazebo overlooking Oriental Lake.

Stag Watching Spots

From North to South:
1. Prince of Wales Shelter
2. Centenary Gazebo
3. Castell Deudraeth Ruins
4. Stone Temple Gazebo
5. Steel Shelter Gazebo
6. Ting Gazebo

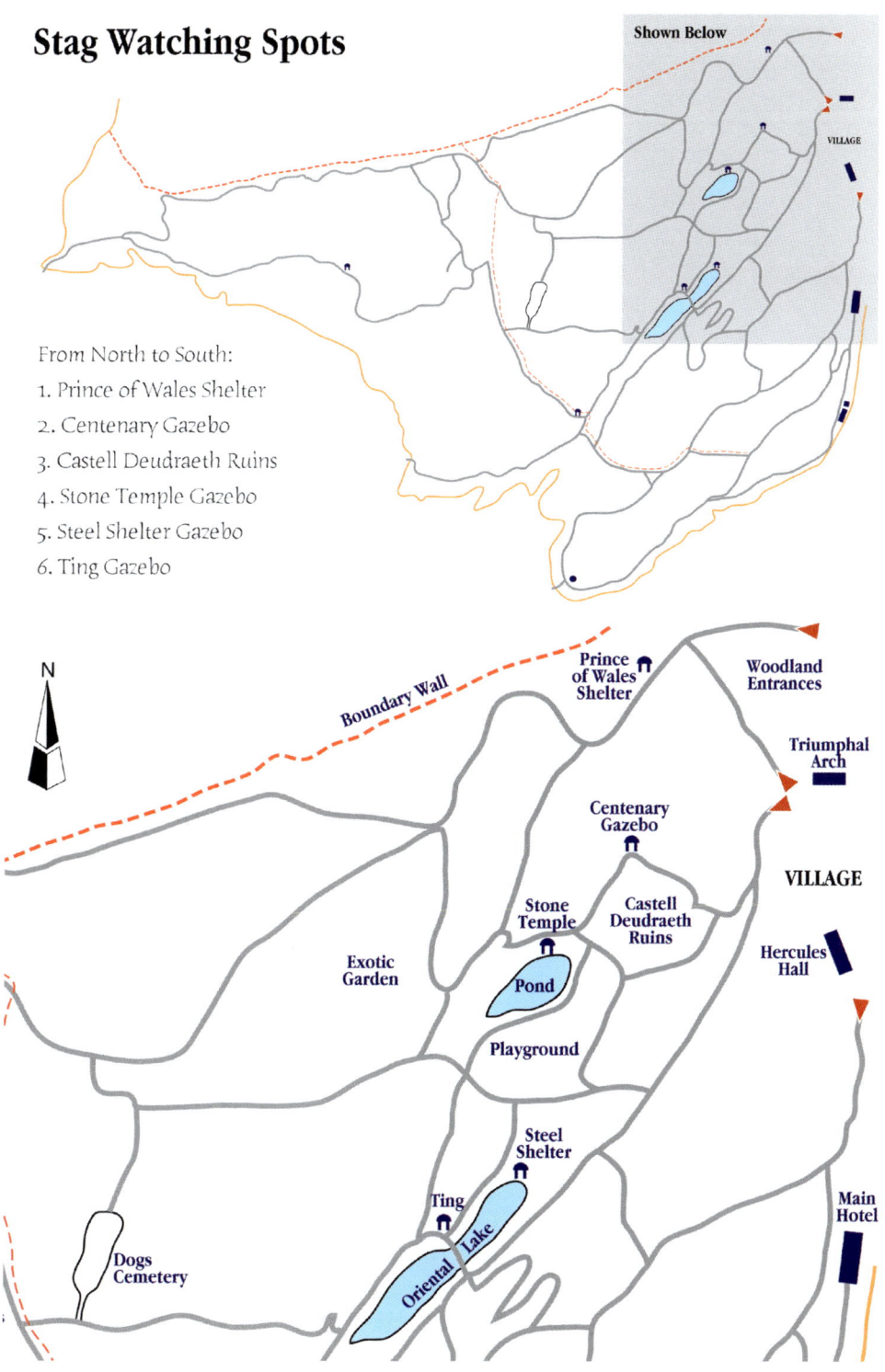

seem to take. Along the way, look for young leaf-buds and bark which have been nibbled off. Listen for a rustling in the foliage. Above all, be prepared for a game of hide-and-seek. One stag watcher related his experience: "The chance of encountering a stag by accident is very small. . . . It is surprising how silently these heavy creatures depart when they are suspicious. Once I heard a stag roll in his mud bath, and yet I could not get a sight of him."[9] It's little wonder the ancient Welshmen considered the stag to be a supernatural creature.

Finally, never attempt to get too near the legendary stag, so as not to startle him. Nor should you attempt to feed him.

The legendary stag of Portmeirion is honored in gold (center) above the entrance to Prior's Lodging.

9   E. N. Buxton, "Timber Creeping in the Carpathians," *Eclectic Magazine* (April 1897)

The legendary stag of Portmeirion is depicted on two sides of an ornamental pot outside Lower Fountain (accessible by overnight guests).

The Huntsman statue at Cliff House. In mythology, the huntsman is, ironically, the stag's ally as well as its adversary. The predator and the prey are mystically united.

On the Tail of a Spectre-Dog

To that Unknown and Silent Shore

> He could hear its faint baying in the hushed night—a ghostly baying that he realized could only come from a ghost dog.
> —Carroll B. Colby, *Scary Stories for Halloween Nights* (2005)

Is there an invisible nether world of ghost animals, where dogs wander about in possession of their spectral life?[1] Where better to ponder such a question than Portmeirion's "Dogs' Cemetery," located at the epicenter of the woodlands. A previous resident of the peninsula, an eccentric woman named Adelaide Haig, buried all of her beloved pets in this forest graveyard. She herself died in 1925, but the tradition has continued through the present day. You'll encounter many tombstones and epitaphs in this eerily quiet place, some so aged or overgrown that their words are difficult to decipher. The grave site

A crossroads near the Dogs' Cemetery in the Woodlands.

---

1   Henry Constable, *Hades* (1873)

of Prince, "our beloved friend who left this world too soon," has a circle of stones around the plot. One of the simplest stones features two words, "Toby Dog," and is encircled by an old leather collar. Other inscriptions include:

> "My dear dear dog gone before
> To that unknown and silent shore
> Shall we not meet as heretofore
> Some summer morning."

> "Mrs. Adelaide Haigh's Dear Dog Jim, once a stray"

> "Pepys, a brave and much-loved cavalier, 1965-1976"

The simple grave marker for "Toby Dog," encircled by an old leather collar.

"Here lies Roger, a faithful friend and companion for 13 years, also much loved son Charlie, 1969"

"Benji—His spirit will remain with us forever."

"Trixie, Loved and Remembered Always, died 29-12-87, aged 15 years"

"Sally, our darling standard poodle. At rest. 13.6.74 - 10.5.89"

"Tammy, a beautiful dog dearly loved, b. 22.2.82, d. 13.11.96, sister of Softy"

"Dearest Darling Woofy, August 1977 - 14.4.94, dearly loved and loving"

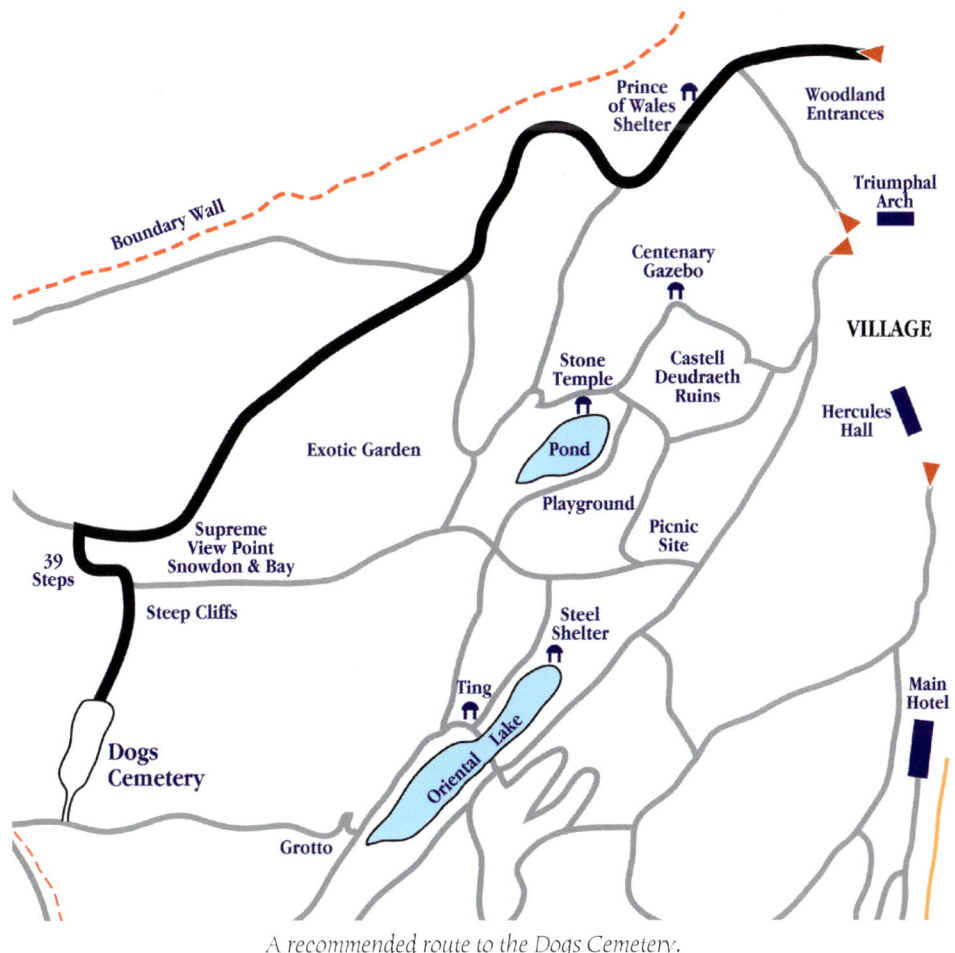

A recommended route to the Dogs Cemetery.

How to Detect a Ghost Dog

With so many dogs buried in this cemetery, the likelihood of ghost presence is exceedingly high. Be aware of the following signs of a canine spectre:

- a sudden chill

- a shadow that seems to keep pace with you

- a barking at one's heels

- the phantasmal appearance of a silent sentinel

- a spine-chilling whimpering or howling

- "eyes like twin golden will-o'-the-wisps in a head of black smoke"[2]

Though undoubtedly eerie, ghost dogs can do no real harm. They cannot bite. On the contrary, they may impart a sense of ease and a feeling of safety, as if a loyal companion is at one's side. Ghost dogs traditionally inhabit lonely places such as cemeteries. They tend to stir at twilight and roam at night, though they may spotted or felt at any time of day.

Identifying the Notorious Spectral Dog of Great Britain

British folklorist T. F. Thiselton Dyer noted that across the United Kingdom "there is a popular belief in a spectral dog, which is generally described as 'large, shaggy, and black, with long ears and tail. It does not belong to any species of living dogs, but is severally said to represent a hound, a setter, a terrier, or a shepherd dog, though often larger than a Newfoundland.' It is commonly supposed to be a bad spirit, haunting places where evil deeds have been done, or where some calamity may be expected." The spectre-dog's feet make a peculiar noise resembling "that of a person walking along a miry, sloppy road, with heavy shoes." The dog is known to utter "a curious screech, which is thought to warn against persons of the approaching death of some relative or friend." When followed, the dog "retreats with its eyes fronting its pursuer, and either sinks into the ground with a frightful shriek, or in some mysterious manner disappears."[3] The Welsh name for these "dogs of hell" is *Cwn Annwn*.

The following spectral dog encounter, from a 1912 guide to Wales[4], describes an area exactly like the northern boundary of the Portmeirion woodlands:

> Several years ago I came very near seeing one of these portentous dogs. I was on a treeless upland pasture, rich with ruby like a deep agate, with lavender, flecked with emerald-green

---

[2] Brian Lumley, *Psychomech* (2001)
[3] T. F. Thiselton Dyer, *The Ghost World* (1893)
[4] Jeannette Augustus Marks, *Gallant Little Wales* (1912)

as musk is freaked with brown; purple, pink, and opalescent in the sunshine that came and went. There were black sheep and white in that pasture, I remember, and some little lambs that straddled with surprise. One rose, stretching and curling its tail with the delicious energy of waking from sleep. I looked down what seemed a particoloured gulf of greensward into valleys where men and cattle had become dots in size, and up to more fern and heather and altitudes where the curlew cried. It was as I looked up that I saw an impressively large black dog that went through an impossibly small sheep-hole in a sheep-wall. But a wisp of mist came over the Welsh mountainside, and one never makes an effort to see that sort of thing or to run after it. Hunting rollicking elves and lightfoot fairies is quite a different matter!

Dogs of the Sky

Welsh legend recounts the Dogs of the Sky (*Cwn y Wybr*), which fly in packs among the clouds in hunt of freshly departed souls. They

The entrance to the woodland Dogs' Cemetery.

are "heard in the dead of night, frightfully yelling over mountain and moor."[5] Here is an account of one sighting that took place back in 1833:

> The devils in shape of hunting dogs fill the vault of heaven with their crying after a soul just loosed from the flesh, eager as our dogs, aye wolf-dogs, ready to be let slip, can be, after the prey, the bloodhounds of passing souls! I saw the rampant fire of each, though I could not see them; that fire which every one goes trailing with him, like a chain, down heaven's steep road to hell; horrid sight! horrid sound! they passed and their yellings died away; and whose soul they caught, for I heard them growl cruelly over some one, I know not; God forbid I should ever know; I fear it was a woman's![6]

The Virtuous Water Dog Apparition

Portmeirion's many streams, ponds, and waterfalls make it the ideal home for a rare spirit known as the "water dog." In the Avesta, the sacred text of Zoroastrianism, the prophet Zarathushtra explains that "At a dog's death his ghost passes down to the great spring under the earth, and there, out of every thousand he-dogs and every thousand she-dogs, is formed a water dog." These dogs are considered especially sacred, indeed ranking as the holiest of all dogs, "and no wonder, when we consider that they possess the virtues of two thousand ordinary dogs such as are good enough for you and me!"[7]

---

5 Samuel Carter Hall, *The Book of South Wales, the Wye, and the Coast* (1861)
6 *The Cambrian Quarterly Magazine and Celtic Repertory*, Vol. V.
7 Alfred P. Sloan, *Dog and Man* (1925)

Gateways to the Spirit World

Ghosts on Winter's Eve

> Some bulk of a ghost in the dark
> Tightens the throat, presses the air to ice.
> —Sally Roberts Jones, "Family Ghost," *Poetry Wales* (1990)

The Triumphal Arch is a prime spirit threshold situated near entrances to the woodlands.

Nos Galan Gaeaf is the Welsh name for All Hallow's Eve (October 31, the night before Winter). Spirits walk abroad on this eve of the ancient Celtic New Year, appearing at midnight on gates and entrances to footpaths.[1] The many gateways of Portmeirion offer first-class locations for ghost watching. The reason is that, as a "home for fallen buildings," Portmeirion's architecture is an appropriation of objects from various cultures, restaged within a new context in order to perform an unresolved allegory "that invoke[s] the ghosts of unclosed histories in a way that allows them to appear as ghosts and reveal the nature of the ambiguous presence."[2] In other words, Portmeirion's

---

1 Peter N. Williams, *Presenting Wales from A to Y* (2003)
2 Jan Verwoert, "Apropos Appropriation," *Tate Triennial 2006*

pastiche allows spectres the ability to present themselves and gives them the opportunity to speak by reviving their dead language.

A golden phoenix flanks a gate near the hotel swimming pool.

The grand Triumphal Arch stands above all other ghost-watching locations, as it serves not only as a threshold to the village but also is situated next to footpaths radiating into the woodlands. The statue at the top of the arch is a caryatid—a maiden dedicated to the moon goddess Artemis.

Other significant thresholds within Portmeirion include:

- The ornate iron gate directly in front of Hercules Hall, with the year 1908 worked into its design

The year 1908 is integrated into the ironwork of the Town Hall gate.

- The iron gate in front of the pink Unicorn cottage, flanked by golden phoenixes

- The trefoil-shaped doorway of the Gloriette, leading into the piazza

- The stone archway leading to the Shell Grotto

- The stone archway near the tollgate, framing a mermaid painted on sheet metal

- The large archway tunnel under the yellow Gate House, above which an ornate emblem reads: "Honi soit qui mal y pense" ("Shame upon him who thinks evil of it")

- The ornate gateway near the hotel swimming pool, crowned by a golden phoenix.

Other Occasions and Spots for Ghost-Watching

Though *Nos Galan Gaeaf* is the classic holiday for spirit sightings, any dark night can do: "In the evening, when the village is closed to the public, guests see the place at is best: peaceful, even ghostly."[3] Overnight residents have the entire village to themselves for uninterrupted ghost watching. As travel critic Vincent Crump describes it, "Once the day-trippers leave, you get all the strangeness to yourself. Stroll through the deserted piazza between pools of pink and purple light, and the illusion of a place not quite of this world is complete."[4]

Christmas Eve is not recommended for ghost-watching, as Welsh lore has it that no evil spirits can appear that night.[5]

During daylight hours, on any day of the year, you're virtually guaranteed to hear eerie whispers in the woodland Ghost Garden.

---

3 Mike Parker and Paul Whitfield, *The Rough Guide to Wales* (2000)
4 "Bolt Hole: Castell Deudraeth, Portmeirion, Gwynedd," TimesOnline (June 27, 2004)
5 Rev. Elias Owen, *Welsh Folk-Lore* (1887)

Which Spirits to Watch For

> Wales has always been noted for its ghosts, fairies and knocking spirits.
> —"A Welsh Ghost," *The Spiritual Magazine* (1868)

A variety of unusual apparitions roam the Welsh countryside, and visitors to Portmeirion are liable to encounter any number of them. Note, however, that according to Welsh lore, if two persons are together, a spirit will be visible to one and invisible to the other. Also, it is said that only one person will hear a spirit speak.

Banshees, the Outcry of Bewildered Souls:
Banshees (*Gwrach y Rhibyn*) are subtle spirits in Snowdonia, easier for the native to discern than the tourist. "The death portents in Cambria reveal all the strangeness and lawlessness of the Celtic imagination. No one who does not know the Welsh hills, who has not been on them day after day, can feel the significance of these death portents. One must have travelled on the top edge of the Welsh mountain world to understand,—have looked out upon a sea of hills gray and barren in

A sign marking the entrance to the woodland Ghost Garden, where rustling Eucalyptus trees carry ghostly whispers.

their utter colourlessness, and down upon valleys like the valley of the shadow of death. There abyss and altitude are alike full of terrors, of mist before which mind and step falter, of an Unknown which presses home in bodily anguish, which distorts the vision and strikes upon the ear with the outcry of bewildered souls. It is not strange, then, that the Welsh have the most horrible of banshees."[6] The Banshee's "gaunt mysterious presence, sweeping over moor and mountain in the pale moonlight, or in the misty darkness, to mourn over the dead of some time-honoured house, becomes almost sublime in its grandeur. The wail is so full of melancholy music, yet so unearthly, that no human creature ever heard it without terror, no animal of the lower world without instinctive trembling. There is no escape from the sound— those who listen to its dismal prelude must hear it to the end." Some believe the Banshee to have been "the foundress of the particular family over whom she mourns; others, that she was appointed their 'follower,' as a reward for some act of fidelity accomplished while in the flesh."[7]

Old Hag of the Mist:
Residing in dripping fog, the ethereal Old Hag of the Mist "is known as the Gwrach y Rhybin. . . . No wonder the peasants cross their doors, even to this day in isolated districts, to shield themselves, and that they keep horseshoes and churchyard earth to preserve their cottages from spells!"[8] Her shrill tenor shriek is believed to foretell misfortune, if not death, to the hearer, especially if she calls one by name.[9]

Corpse Candles:
The pale bluish light of a Corpse Candle (*Canwyll Corph*) flickers on dark lanes or in houses shortly before a fatal event. They move "slowly and steadily towards graves that are about to receive occupants. They vary in brilliancy and size, according to the age and growth of the party doomed: sometimes there are two—one large, the other small; a mother and child are sure to die somewhere in the neighborhood, whenever these two candles are encountered."[10]

---

6   Jeannette Augustus Marks, *Gallant Little Wales* (1912)
7   Samuel Carter Hall, *The Book of South Wales, the Wye, and the Coast* (1861)
8   Jeannette Augustus Marks, *Gallant Little Wales* (1912)
9   Rev. Elias Owen, *Welsh Folk-Lore* (1887)
10 Samuel Carter Hall, *The Book of South Wales, the Wye, and the Coast* (1861)

White Lady:
The White Lady is a shining spectre who "haunts the burial-place of hidden treasure, and who, having selected some individual to whom to reveal its whereabouts, never gives him rest till she has accomplished her purpose. She suddenly appears—a bright vision—clothed in white, with her glossy, coal-black locks dishevelled over her shoulders; her face is pale and careworn, and wears an expression of intense pain. She never speaks to mortal man, but by signs indicates what she has to communicate. Though perfectly harmless, indeed frequently of great service, she is an object of much fear to the neighborhood she haunts, and to him she has chosen as an unwilling confidant. One man who occupied such a position informed us, that for years he had no peace night or day for her. She appeared to him with an agonizing expression of countenance, at unexpected times, and in unexpected places. Once, in a field to which there were several entrances, she appeared and opposed his exit. Trembling he sought another, but there too was she. He fainted, and did not leave the field, till he was found there by persons who happened to pass. At last, some considerable amount of jewels and other valuables was found by the man, who is a carpenter, in the secret drawer of an old escritoir, which he was repairing for a family that resided near. The valuables were immediately handed over to the owner of the escritoir, and the 'White Lady' has not since appeared."[11]

Corpse Birds:
The *Aderyn y Corph* is an underworld owl which screeches at the door or window of a person who is about to die.[12]

Listless Ghosts:
There are plenty of ghosts to be found in Wales, "but they are rather spiritless creatures, much easier to catch and not so tricksy as the fairies. Nor do they select prickly furze and stony hilltops as their hiding-places. But on the whole they are difficult to subdue."[13]

Satan:
"The visible appearance of his satanic majesty we have found rather

---

11 Samuel Carter Hall, *The Book of South Wales, the Wye, and the Coast* (1861)
12 Wirt Sikes, *British Goblins* (1881)
13 Jeannette Augustus Marks, *Gallant Little Wales* (1912)

prevalent in Wales. Sometimes he manifests himself in a ball of fire, which suddenly falls at the feet of the wayfarer, explodes, and then disappears, leaving a strong smell of sulphur behind. At other times he assumes the form of a donkey, and very frequently that of a black calf. Certain places are sacred to him in each of these forms. Where he is once seen as a ball of fire, he is never after seen as a calf, and vice versá."[14]

Cyhyraeth:
This groaning, worm-eaten spectral woman "moans dolefully in the night but is never seen."[15] She is believed to weep before a death or to herald a disaster. Her cry is "generally heard by some person nearly related to the person doomed; it proceeds from the house in which lies the sick, and stops at the place of burial. These cries are warnings, and ought to be taken as such."[16]

Torrent Spectre:
This malignant spirit appears as an old man and rules over mountain torrents. Horrible to behold, with long hair standing on end, he raises himself half out of a rushing stream, then ascends "like a mist half as high as the near mountain."[17]

Tolaeth:
This knocking spirit "groans or sings or saws, or tramps with its feet and is also unseen."[18] The rappings resemble the noise made by a carpenter when engaged in coffin-making.[19]

Goblin Funerals:
The Welsh name for goblin funerals is *Teulu*. "Cases are very numerous where funerals of shadows have been seen on roads to church-yards,—sure heralds of deaths,—and of processions of actual mourners, proceeding on the same road a few weeks afterwards." These midnight spectral processions feature the doleful singing of Welsh funeral

---

14 Samuel Carter Hall, *The Book of South Wales, the Wye, and the Coast* (1861)
15 Jeannette Augustus Marks, *Gallant Little Wales* (1912)
16 Samuel Carter Hall, *The Book of South Wales, the Wye, and the Coast* (1861)
17 Rev, Elias Owen, *Welsh Folk-Lore* (1887)
18 Jeannette Augustus Marks, *Gallant Little Wales* (1912)
19 Rev, Elias Owen, *Welsh Folk-Lore* (1887)

hymns, "the rustling of dresses, the hum of voices, and even the breathing of persons passing close by."[20]

An Ethereal Wishing Well

Considering that Portmeirion is comprised of "bits and pieces from disintegrating stately mansions,"[21] it may come as little surprise that some of its ghosts are actually concrete. Following is a true account[22] we might call "Mortar and Mater" or "Nooks and Grannies."

A concrete ghost. This eerily-lit phantom turret appears on the piazza in this accidental double-exposure (with light leak). Photograph by Anthony Brierley.

---

20 Samuel Carter Hall, *The Book of South Wales, the Wye, and the Coast* (1861)
21 Abigail Hole and Etail O'Carroll, *Wales* (2004)
22 P. S. Gifford, "Travelogue: A Haunting Memory," CastleOfSpirits.com (2005)

In April 2004, P. S. Gifford traveled with his wife, Sarah, and eleven year old son, Jonathan, from their home in California back to his native Great Britain. Upon arriving at his ancestral house, Gifford dug out a shoebox collection of old faded childhood photos and tearfully pored over them for nearly an hour. He carefully placed several especially sentimental ones into his wallet, then set off with his family for a tour of Wales.

Their first stop was Portmeirion, on an idyllic, cloudless day. They lazily explored the charming architecture, then delighted in relaxing strolls along the estuary. While enjoying noon tea and admiring the view from the bakery, Gifford noticed something intriguing:

> an old wishing-well, some distance away from the center of the town, and entangled within some seemingly primordial vines on a patch of overgrown grass. It looked curiously out of place within the neatly trimmed gardens, so upon finishing my tea we decided that a closer look was in order, and with my son keenly at my heels, we eagerly approached it. It was so unusual that I decided to take a photograph and posed Jonathan comically in front of it. A few moments later, as we were walking away, I casually tossed a penny over my right shoulder, and as I heard a splash of acknowledgement and gratitude from the old well, I closed my eyes tightly and made a wish.

During their final hour in the village, Jonathan begged to explore an old stone path leading to the beach. Sarah decided to wait on a well-worn bench at the top of the rocks, admiring the view from a safe and comfortable distance as her husband and son dared their way down to the golden sands. Twenty minutes later, they reemerged and, huffing for breath, happily collapsed next to Sarah on the bench. Gifford recalls:

> I asked her if she had been all right whilst we had been gone, and she replied joyfully that a peculiar experience had occurred during our absence, as that not one minute after we had set off she had gotten some company. A sweet middle aged lady, with the face of an angel, had come

and sat next to her. She went on to inform me that she presumed the lady was lonely and visiting by herself, and that they soon comfortably fell into a deep conversation. It was strange, my wife continued, explaining how they talked as if knowing each other for years. In fact, she told me the delightful lady had only left moments before my return, or I would have gotten to meet her for myself.

Jonathan interrupted the conversation, asking for money to buy some ice creams. Gifford's wallet was inside his wife's hand bag; as Sarah reached in to retrieve the money, something made her gasp. One of Gifford's old family photos had fallen out. His wife was staring wide-eyed at a picture of Gifford's deceased mother. Sarah whispered in disbelief: "That was the woman I was chatting with!"

Gifford's mind raced at the surprising revelation:

> Since discovering those photographs, I had become obsessed with the fact that the two most important women in my life had never met. I had been dreaming of just how well they would have gotten along together. In fact, I had been dwelling about it so much that when I had tossed that penny into the well, I had wished that the two of them had met.

After their vacation, Gifford searched for the photo he snapped of the old wishing well. He was startled to discover that it depicted his son—and nothing more.

Subtle Hauntings

Three Omnipresent Forces

Portmeirion is ever-haunted by three inescapable spectres. Their presence is readily evident with the slightest perceptual shift, just as in the classic "Vase or Two Silhouetted Faces" optical illusion. The spectres are:

- Traditional Welsh architecture. Portmeirion is (and was intended to be) a national aberration. The simple, sober, functional, and slate-colored style of Wales looms over Portmeirion like a storm cloud, held back by the sheer force of its own disbelief.

The sea and woodlands encroach on the Portmeirion hotel.

- Mother Nature. Portmeirion seeks to offer hospitality in an inhospitable place. The wild woodlands fight to take back the peninsula. The encroaching sea and unflagging wind would (and will, eventually) shape the rugged cliffs according to their own whims.

- Modernity.

> It contains not only the clutter and dust of history but also, the ghosts that the modern would deny: the ghosts of modernity itself.
> —Calum Storrie, *The Delirious Museum* (2006)

Fairies Underfoot

Traces of Enchantment

Folklorist Jeannette Augustus Marks notes that the Welsh speak of the little people as "fair folk" or family–"γ Tylwyth Teg." Sometimes they are called "fair folk of the wood" or "of the mine." In size, they are no bigger than an agate stone, as Shakespeare described. Marks suggests looking for fairies as they dance on moonlit nights "in gowns of green, blue, white, and scarlet.... If they like you they will bestow blessings on you, and are frequently called 'mothers' blessings' because mothers are glad to have such little ones. But if one speaks unkindly of them, one will get into trouble."[1]

Marks says that "the essence of all that is Celtic is the Welsh fairy." She assures us that "The real fairy is still in Wales, and if you do not believe me, all I can say is, that you must go to Wales and prove that I am wrong. But perhaps it would be well before you take the journey to look at your foot, for if you find you have not a foot that water runs under, it is best for you not to go. So runs the ancient proverb, and without that lucky foot no fairy shall you see."

Marks recalls her first eerie fairy encounter, in a location very near Portmeirion:

> It was dusk, and I had come through a tiny hill village, where white cottages were gleaming in the dark, and light shining on garden walls. It was so quiet that I could hear pine needles dropping on the ground, and the wind talking in the branches of the rain, still miles distant upon the sea. The noise of a tardy bumblebee, hurrying homeward in the dark, fairly boomed in my ears, and the sounds of shale rock slipping down the hillside came and went mysteriously. Through lighted windows I caught glimpses of evening comfort, of a bright fire glowing with peat, whose aroma was everywhere on the soft air, of dressers and

---

1   *Gallant Little Wales* (1912.)

A cliffside fairy doorway (center) in the Portmeirion woodlands.

A tree root fairy doorway (lower left) in the Portmeirion woodlands.

tridarns, brave with countless ornaments, of a grandfather's clock whose wise old face shone with light, of children's heads about the supper table.

But a higher hill was calling me, and an adventure of whose nature I had not even dreamed. I turned off the road by a Wesleyan chapel and mounted a steep path. Up, up, up I went around the side of a green hill, sometimes listening to the night stir of the birds, sometimes startled by a brown rabbit, leaping for cover. Out beyond, the mountains of Snowdonia were piled height on height, all washed in sepia depth upon a sky, moonless, but brilliant with stars. I hastened, for I was eager to reach the pine-crowned summit. Up there would be no sound except the wind in the trees, and once in a while some homely noises from the villages in the valley below: the sharp bark of a dog, the bleating of a lamb, the closing of some cottage door, a resonant "good-night."

Once upon the hilltop, I lay down to rest, listening to the soft flight and hooting of some young owl, and feeling the grass cool and deep to my head and hands. As I lay there, eyes half closed, I heard some one coming up the path. Nearer and nearer drew uncertain footsteps and the tapping of a cane over loose stones. I sat up quickly, and there in the dark was an old woman, a cane in one hand, a basket in the other. Something cried piteously from the basket and I asked what it was. The old crone said that it was a kitten, and showed me a sack in which something else, tied up, squirmed and mewed. But she did not open the bag. After a due amount of greeting and curtseying, the old woman went on. I noticed that she kept looking back as she followed the path over the crown of the hill.

My attention was diverted from her by the approach of more footsteps. It was a boy, a very large boy, and in his hand I could clearly see a school-bag, ridiculously small for such a big lad, in which he, too, carried something. Behind him walked a huge dog, feathered on back and legs so heavily that his shaggy hair trailed on the ground. I heard something cry from the little bag, and I asked what it was. The lad replied in Welsh that it was a kitten. I could see him smiling as he stood his ground. Except in Welsh there was nothing further for me to do. Under the most favourable circumstances it is a great deal to anything at all in Welsh, and with my heart beating rapidly and my tongue growing dry, I did not feel that I could do anything more in any language. We were silent while the little thing kept on "miaowing," and this boy, like an ordinary boy, hitched about for a few moments, kicking stones from the path, and then went on, followed by the dog.

Erect and uneasy, I continued to sit up. Just as dog and boy were out of sight I heard some one else stumbling up the path and a faint kitten-like noise. I began to be afraid of those kittens being carried one after one over this desolate hilltop. It suggested a little the enchantments in the "Mabinogion," only in the "Mabinogion" mice and not kittens played the leading part. I got up and fled before this experience should have a chance to become the beginning of some enchantment. But already I felt as if a spell were upon me, and even when I was quite far away from the kitteny place, I was still in a strange condition of excitement. One feels a natural dislike for any sort of hilltop enchantments, as I did.

I was making considerable speed in my Welsh-soled boots and feeling more like an ordinary person, when the path took a sharp turn and I saw something strange in front of me. Down below ran the road, hard enough to be a fact, and lighted by the clear glow of the stars. If only one could always be sure of what is coming in this world, such a turning as I had taken would be like Keats's beauty, "a joy forever." But alas! close at my own right hand, very distinct, unmistakably clear, rose something my eyes had never met before: a chimney with no house attached to it. And on the treeless meadow in front of this apparition I saw the old woman leaning on her stick and the boy sitting beside his dog. Clearly the spell had worked. But how I struggled out from under this enchantment is another story.

A fairy doorway (center) in a moss-covered rocky outcropping in the Portmeirion woodlands.

Modern accounts of fairy sightings are most often dismissed outright. "No one who has not seen a fairy can have any idea how difficult it is to draw the line between history and story," Marks notes. "The difficulties of the folklorist are as nothing,—for his is the scientific spirit,—compared with the trouble the real fairy hunter has in the open. Nowadays, of course, no one believes everything or possibly anything he is told."

A Tricky Nature

Welsh fairies can be relied upon to be tricksters, Marks says. "They not only have a rather practical-joking sort of humour, but they also have very little sense of equity. A man may do his best for them, and then they repay him in the end by a trick." Marks recounts a story that could easily have taken place in the woodlands of Portmeirion:

> A Welsh piper was coming home in the gray of the evening, and had to cross a little running stream, from which he saw only the shadowed hillside and heard only the voice of the wind. But when he had travelled beyond the hill, music became audible, and, turning, instead of the knoll he had been looking at, there was a great castle with lights blazing and music playing and the sound of dancing feet. He went back and was caught in the procession coming out from its doors and taken in to pipe to them. He piped for a day or so, but he was anxious to return to his people, and the fairies seemed to understand. They said they would let him go if he would play a favourite tune. He played his best, they danced fast and furiously. And at last he was set free on the dark hillside, with only the voice of the wind for company. He went home hastily, but when he entered his father's house no one knew him. An old man awake from a doze by the fire, and said that he had heard, when a boy, of a piper who had gone away on a quiet evening and never come back again. That was over a hundred years ago.

Marks suggests that we not judge the fairies too harshly. "Perhaps there is no reason why the fairies, as well as poor mortals, should not be allowed a natural and happy alternation between badness and goodness. Metaphorically speaking, they are not the only creatures who steal money and butter and cheese, and who whisk away helpless, unbaptized infants."

The Importance of Welsh Cheese

"There is only one thing that can possibly counteract the lack of a requisite instep for those who desire to see fairies," Marks notes, "and that is eating a good deal of cheese. I do not know why this is, but I do know that as far back as one can go, much further back than Giraldus Cambrensis or even Taliessin or the archest of the arch-druids, Welsh rarebit and roasted cheese have been the very bread of Cymric diet. There is a story in John Rastell's 'Hundred Mery Talys,' printed in the sixteenth century, which shows that before Shakespeare came to elucidate the Welsh fairy, this question of cheese and the Welsh had been duly considered." Rastell holds that when a great company of Welshmen approached the Kingdom of Heaven, their babbling wearied God. Saint Peter went to Heaven's gate and loudly cried *caws pob* ("roasted cheese"). The Welshmen ran away at a great pace as Saint Peter locked the gate. "Undoubtedly among everything Welsh, even in literature, cheese is the 'Open Sesame.' ... Is there any other folk-lore in the history of the world in which cheese plays so important a role? It might in German folk-lore, but the fact is that it does not. Bread, milk, the juice of the grape, but cheese? No, that is lifted into the realm of imagination and of a world-classic only in Cambria. Again Shakespeare showed his surprisingly accurate knowledge of the Celt when Falstaff exclaims, 'Heaven defend me from that Welsh Fairy, lest he transform me into a piece of cheese!'"

A Portrait of the Artist as Portmeirion

A Personal Expression of a Peculiar Genius

A self-portrait reveals an artist's unique personality and character. If we consider Portmeirion to be Clough Williams-Ellis's grand self-portrait, what does it reveal about him?

Clough began designing his self-portrait in childhood. From the age of five or six, he knew that some day he would build a village "that would body forth my chafing ideas of fitness and gaiety and indeed *be me*."[1] After he considered purchasing one of 22 islands, he ended up with land only five miles from his own home. "No man is an island," as John Donne said, and Clough found that his independent spirit could in fact find expression within the domain of his ancestors.

Nicholas De Jongh notes in *Crawdaddy* that Clough was a rebel and a revolutionary. "He was born into the British upper classes and left them as soon as he could. . . . [H]is memorial and his dream, both alive in his own lifetime, is something which has nothing to do with the conformity or order of his own breed of people. Most surprisingly, he's out of harmony with most of the architects of this century who have timidly plunged the new world into an infinity of sameness, with boxes and concrete the governing motifs."

In the prologue to *Portmeirion: The Place and Its Meaning*, Christopher Hussey says this about the village: "Actually, it is a personal expression of Mr. Ellis's peculiar genius. A Welshman himself, he has an instinct for the handling of the rough local materials and a deep feeling for what his landscape can assimilate. Thus controlled, his luxuriant imagination and somewhat flamboyant tastes find a perfect exercise in such a creation as this. With all its ebullience and gaiety and joyous

---

1 *Portmeirion: The Place and Its Meaning.*

Sculptor Jonah Jones crafted Clough into the very stonework of the Bristol Colonnade. Clough's self-portrait in Portmeirion itself reveals a cheerful outlook, the eyes of a child, a rebel, a revolutionary, a nonconformist, a naturalist, flamboyance, and peculiar genius.

freakishness, Portmeirion is essentially of the soil, and every part bears the authentic touch of the artist."

Imagine that the village is a giant relief map of Clough. His every feature is represented in some way. Wander around the village and locate the following features:

- Heart
- Eyes
- Mouth
- Ears
- Soul
- Fingers
- Arms
- Feet
- Backbone

Some possible soul features:

Toll House St. Peter: Building Upon Wisdom

Lion Statue: Sovereign

Buddha Loggia: Harmonious

Cherub Below Pantheon: Supportive of Nature

Steps to the estuary: Clough's backbone?

Woodland lookout point: Clough's fingers?

Portmeirion as a House of Tarot Cards

Interactive Archetypes

Imagine a well-shuffled Tarot deck formulating the blueprint for this eccentric village, every picture unfolding into picturesque architecture, every background transforming into real ground, every portent a literal signpost. Indeed, Portmeirion is like a Tarot deck made manifest in mortar and gold leaf. Around one corner, a statue of a cherubic Fool stands blithely on the edge of a rocky precipice. Down another

path, the World sits atop the shoulders of a Hercules statue, while the God-Empress Frigga looks on. Elsewhere, St. Peter pontificates from a balcony like a true Hierophant, in the shadow of a soaring Tower. Taken together, the assorted facets of Portmeirion are eerily like an elaborate spread of divinatory cards—an esoteric pop-up book of sorts in which all 22 major archetypes interrelate in three dimensions.

With its structures cascading down a lofty cliffside, the village's winding, stepped paths of varying elevations provide innumerable vantage points to study the relative iconic connections. Archetypes may be adjacent or separate, above or below one another, all depending upon one's standpoint. The village can be viewed as one elaborate allegorical story, told from multiple perspectives. As Tarot scholar L. W. De Laurence noted, allegory and symbol are inclusive of all nations and times. Hence, "the cards correspond to many types of ideas and things; they are universal and not particular."[1] As Portmeirion is a pastiche of architecture and ornaments from different cultures and eras, it's a uniquely perfect setting for the Tarot archetypes to spring into life.

Like all works of art, the statues, paintings, and architecture of Portmeirion find their meanings in the beholder's interpretation. Is the concrete planter emblazoned with a relief of a trident-wielding King Neptune a reflection of the King of Cups? Do the two Balinese dancers atop Ionic columns in the piazza epitomize the Two of Wands? Visitors must come to their own terms, according to the context of their situation and the call of intuition. Following is a proposed representation of the Major Arcana at play within Portmeirion, to serve as an inspiration to the unconventional traveler eager to read the signs and portents all around.

The Major Arcana

The Fool stands within the crevice of a dramatic rocky outcropping, above and behind the Bristol Colonnade. It's as if he has already taken one fall and is unaware that his next step will be another big one. His right hand is raised over his head in a devil-may-care gesture. Perhaps he is pointing high above, to the turret-like Chantry Outlook,

---

1 *The Key to the Tarot* (1918)

distinguished by a tall stone column supporting a weather vane. It seems likely that this is where the Fool has been. Has he reached too high in the past? Is he still lost in the clouds?

The Magician is a bronze bust of the wizard who envisioned and manifested Portmeirion as his retirement hobby. Clough literally created his village out of thin air (or at least thin dust): as he couldn't afford building materials, he salvaged bits and pieces of "fallen buildings" and reconstructed them according to his alchemical whim. The bust is molded in rough style, as if clay had hurriedly been formed into a golem and then cast in metal just as its eyes opened. Framed by an arch, the Magician is located in the entryway to Hercules Hall.

The High Priestess is the *trompe l'oeil* mermaid "sculpture" painted on sheet metal. She sports two tails, symbolizing duality. They curl up to suggest, along with her curved arms, a figure-eight/infinity shape. The infinity shape is echoed in the dramatic curls of her hair. Eyes closed, she cradles a large fish from whose mouth flows the water of the deep realm of the unconscious. The High Priestess, framed by an archway, meditatively sits atop a sphere in a stone pavilion near the tollgate.

The Empress is a statue of the Nordic all-mother Goddess Frigga (labeled "Frix" on the plinth), ruler of love, marriage, and fertility. Wielding a crossbow in her left hand and the hilt of a sword in the other, the Empress stands assuredly atop a limestone pedestal, head turned toward her right. She is framed by greenery and overlooks the small fountain between the Mermaid and Dolphin cottages. The fountain is a popular wishing well, establishing the Empress as a heeder of prayers and granter of desires. Her broken sword (presumably ruined over time) is of interest, as it symbolizes a firm grip on intention, free from lacerations.

The Emperor is a colorful statue along the estuary, at the foot of the Observatory Tower. The statue honors Admiral Lord Nelson, hero of

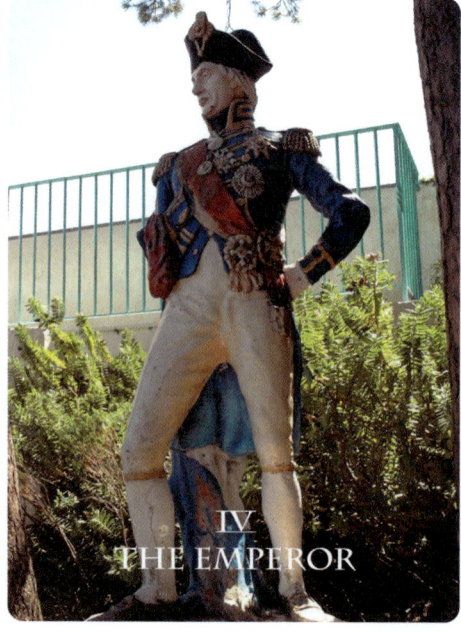

the Napoleonic Wars. He stands powerfully, in full regalia. As we have noted, the Observatory Tower houses Portmeirion's camera obscura, whose submarine lens offers clandestine panoramic views of the village and estuary. As the projected image is upside down and backward, a new perspective would seem to afford the "big picture."

The Hierophant is a statue of a bearded St. Peter, preaching from an ironwork balcony. His right hand gestures as he reads from a scroll. He wears a blue toga over a red robe. Above his head dangles a funnel-like green parasol, reminiscent of a gramophone horn. It's as if a heavenly audio signal is being directed toward his head. The Hierophant sermonizes from above the shop at the Toll House. On the wall to his right is a bell (originally used to summon the village gatekeeper) and striped pole (historically lowered to restrict access). These features establish the Hierophant as an intermediary, a threshold guardian and an opener of doors.

The Lovers are depicted in a Classical-style ceiling mural beneath the archway of the Gate House. The figures are pagan deities, reminiscent of ancient zodiacal personages at play in the heavens. Acrobatically tumbling through the ethers, one figure atop a horse reaches out to

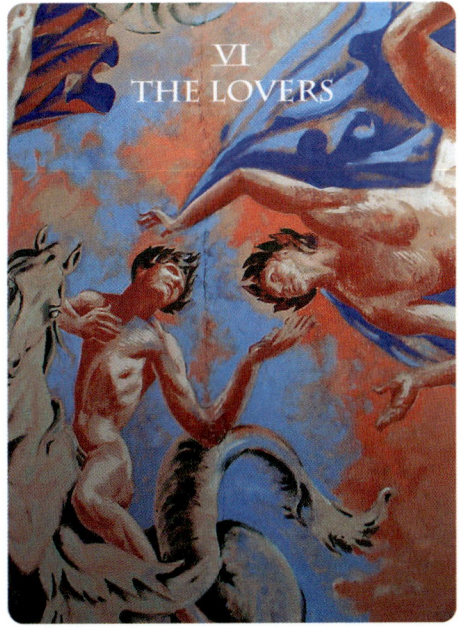

join hands with another whose cape billows like a parachute. Though their fingers haven't yet touched, their eyes are locked. The composition suggests a Yin/Yang balance and a clockwise cyclical flow.

The Chariot is an enormous clamshell which carries a majestic Triton reminiscent of Poseidon. With his right hand he holds a nautiloid shell trumpet to his lips. He brandishes a trident in his left hand. The base of the trident dips into the sea like a rudder, suggesting a three-pronged maneuver. The Triton sports two tails which splash behind him, symbolic of motion without external propulsion. He faces forward, sounds his horn to his right, and points his eyes and trident leftward. Vigilance, preparedness, and assertion are indicated. The Chariot is painted on the back of the Bristol Colonnade.

Strength is the lion statue, regally lying under a hedgerow canopy behind the Gothic Pavilion. The lion is awake but restful, his jaw relaxed and his eyes simultaneously fixed and glazed, as if in the midst of mindful meditation. As the statue was a 90th birthday present to Portmeirion's founder, it suggests strength through endurance, resilience, life-long learning, and legacy.

The Hermit stands in a lofty alcove, right hand clutching his heavy cloak, right knee bent to take a step. Above his head a large five-pointed starburst illuminates his way. Yet, with eyes closed, the Hermit appears to take guidance from an inner light. He is located above an archway to the piazza, near the fish pond. Interestingly, his back is to the pond, as if his journey has taken him out from the depths of the unconscious. Perhaps his eyes haven't yet adjusted to the light of the intellect.

The Wheel of Fortune is actually several bands on perpendicular axes, intersecting to create an armillary sphere. The celestial circles are crowned by a corkscrew drill bit, symbolic of a higher purpose. The Wheel of Fortune's composition suggests cyclical movement. All elements are in play: the armillary sits atop a white column (Air) on the outlook platform of the Shell Grotto (Earth), overlooking the Portmeirion Hotel on the estuary (Water) and facing the setting sun (Fire).

Justice is the statue of a dispassionate angel wearing a long white robe. Her two hands unroll a ribbon-like scroll. Balance is suggested by the positions of her hands: she raises the left end of the scroll almost above her head, while the right hand is fully extended downward. Justice stands on a pedestal in the middle of the Bristol Colonnade.

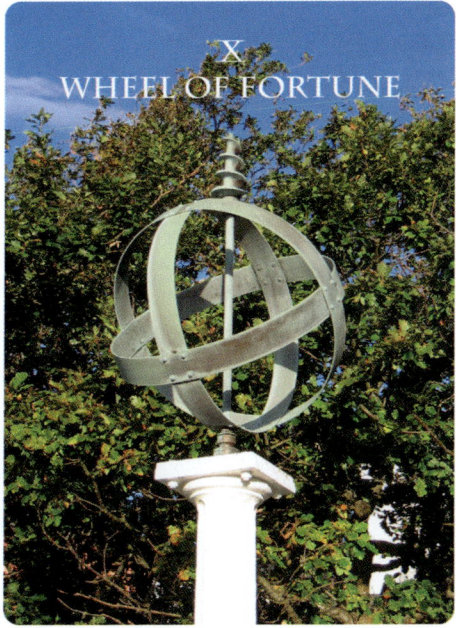

The Hanged Man is a black sheep limply dangling from a balcony. Formed of cut sheet metal, the ram is a silhouette of itself, its only dimensionality provided by its curled white horns. The darkness and flatness suggest an encounter with the shadow self. Suspension of will is explicit—the limpness symbolizes an end to struggle, a relinquishment, an acceptance. As a silhouette in profile, the sheep's two eyes have become one, and that eye is wide open to experience nonduality. The Hanged Man is located on the side of Toll House, just below the St. Peter statue.

Death is in the form of an eagle clutching a snake in its talons. The eagle's wings are spread triumphantly as it lands with its prey upon a

sphere, balanced atop a shell-embellished cube, propped by a green column. Precariousness is made manifest in this arrangement. The eagle of Death is located in the center of Battery Square.

Temperance is the golden statue of a meditating Buddha. As we noted, the Buddha's right arm is missing from the elbow down. The missing arm symbolizes sacrificial measures toward self-restraint. The Buddha of Temperance is located in the pantiled loggia below the looming dome of the Pantheon. Whereas a pantheon is traditionally dedicated to all deities, this Buddha statue is set apart in a lowly place to pursue self-realization.

The Devil is a legendary red wyvern. It sports a barbed serpent's tail, dragon-like wings, and eagle's talons. Wyverns symbolize strife, envy, and pestilence, yet their association with strength and endurance has earned a noble place in medieval heraldry. The Devil is located near the Portmeirion Hotel, above the steps leading to the shore of the estuary. The Devil also appears in a window of Government House (not visible to day visitors).

The Tower is the striking Campanile that rises above the entire

village. As discussed earlier, it is partially constructed from the ruins of the 12th century Castell Deudraeth, impiously razed in the 19th century so as not to attract tourism. Hence, the cycle of creation, destruction, and recreation is embodied in the Tower.

The Star surmounts the Observatory Tower. Its eight points shine in gold, symbolically providing light for the "fairy images" of the camera obscura within. The Star, then, illuminates the shadowy confines of one's vision not with mere light but with inspiring panoramic reflections.

The Moon and the *Sun* represent themselves at Portmeirion, their shining forms frequently framed by archways and portals. However,

two statues within the village are associated with these heavenly bodies. At the top of the Triumphal Arch is a caryatid—a maiden dedicated to the moon goddess Artemis. And a cherub balances a sundial on his head at the steps to the Bristol Colonnade. The sun and moon are also depicted inside the ground floor of the Campanile, the moon painted on the ceiling and the sun in tile on the floor.

Judgement is a *trompe l'oeil* painting of a winged angel standing upon the little globe of Earth. With both hands she holds a great trumpet to her lips, and she sounds it with eyes closed. The angel is surrounded by three eight-pointed stars, a golden crown, and a ribbon-like halo of white and blue. Judgement is located on one side of Angel Cottage.

The World is the statue of Hercules (representing Atlas) supporting the Earth. The World is located near Hercules Hall, at the top of Hercules Steps. As we noted earlier, attached to the base of the statue are several engraved tablets, commemorating various splendid years and spinning the flow of time into a whirlpool. Hence, The World speaks of timeless contentment.

The Minor Arcana

The suits of the Minor Arcana appear throughout Portmeirion, too. Cups are represented by numerous vases and fonts. The Three of Cups, for example, could be the dolphin fountain in the Shell Grotto with three clamshell reservoirs. Wands are represented by multitudinous columns, appearing singularly as well as in sets. The Queen of Wands, for example, could be

reflected in the Victorian-era figurehead atop the ornamental petrol pump outside Neptune Cottage. Swords gleam in the village ironwork. The Ace of Swords, for example, could be the iron protrusion atop a stone pillar of the ruined outlook in the woodlands. Pentacles are reflected in slate paving discs, circular windows, and other round motifs. The Five of Pentacles, for example, could be the walkway outside Angel Cottage.

A *Sample Reading*

The intrepid traveler could use any snapshot from Portmeirion as the basis of a three-dimensional Tarot reading. If a friend or loved one appears in the photo, he or she will stand as the querent. The Tarot archetypes within the frame will constitute the spread. Icons just around the corner, hovering in the background, or partially obscured from view may lend insight into emerging or receding trends.
By way of example, consider a snapshot featuring the Campanile on the left (the Tower), the Frigga statue in the center (the Empress),

and the Hercules statue on the right (the World). Down the walkway just out of view is the lion statue (Strength). In three dimensional space, the World is at the forefront, turning in the general direction of the Empress. The Empress looks to her right, toward the hidden lion of Strength. The Tower looms in the background. In this three-dimensional spread, the World spotlights the completion of a cycle. Hercules has accomplished the goal of his struggle. He rotates toward the Empress, ruler over an emerging feminine energy characteristic of the next cycle. The direction of her gaze (toward the lion statue) suggests that hidden strengths will soon be called upon. As the Tower is partially obscured by trees in the background, it appears that the time of crisis is over, even though its shadow may yet have a chilling effect.

Portmeirion means something different to every visitor, but each archway framing a view and each intriguing statue in an alcove invites mindful appreciation. Those with even a rudimentary knowledge of the Tarot will have a field day assimilating the whimsical symbols at play.

Scavenger Hunt: Golden Buddha's Missing Arm

An Unusual Statue

Portmeirion's Buddha statue is notable for several reasons. It was originally a film prop, created for *Inn of the Sixth Happiness* (1958). It now sits in a half-shelter, half-cave, partially glowing in the sunlight and partially obscured by shadows. Its right arm is missing from the elbow down.

Somewhere within the village are:

• a severed right arm, in stone

• a severed right hand, in wood

• a red hand print.

Can you find all three? (Answers on the following pages.)

The Buddha statue is situated below the Pantheon dome.

Answers to the scavenger hunt for Buddha's missing arm. Above, a severed stone arm is protected by the lion statue near the tollgate. Next page, a red hand print (the Red Hand of Ulster) figures into the coat of arms above the doorway to Town Hall, and an enormous wooden hand sits atop a stump in the woodlands.

Scavenger Hunt: The Architect's Signature

Sign on the Dotted Blueprint Line

The study of graphology seeks to reveal a person's character from his or her handwriting. What do you observe about Clough's signature below?

Note the following unique characteristics:

- The underline denotes a justified sense of importance and taking responsibility. This line seems to serve as a sort of foundation for the signature.

- The lasso- or hook-like *E* indicates a desire to keep things under one's own control.

- The capital *C* also reflects a tendency to enclose and control. It literally surrounds the other letters in the first name.

- The lines of the *m* are not connected, signifying one who follows his own inclinations and who is imaginative, inventive, intuitive, self-reliant, and perhaps stubborn.

- The first name and last name are connected with a bold line, indicating an integrated personality.

- This same connecting line also establishes a sort of roof over the *W*, sheltering the middle word.

- A diminutive hyphen connects *Clough* to *Williams*, just as a bolder hyphen connects *Williams* to *Ellis*. This reveals a tendency to incorporate separate parts into an interrelated whole.

- In one of the most unusual features of the signature, the dot of the *i* in *Ellis* seems to have a reflection below it.

An idiograph is a mark or signature characteristic of a particular person. Clough certainly left his mark on Portmeirion. As you stroll around the village, try to identify elements of Clough's signature. For example, is Hercules holding up the dot of an *I* pedestal? Is another dot at the top of the Campanile, or at the top of the lighthouse? Where is an *I* dot reflected?

Scavenger Hunt: On the Tails of the Wild Sea-Fairies

The Song of Half-Human Monsters

> Two long slimy tails, like an eel's, that are roll'd
> And twisted, and shining in silver and gold.
> "'Tis a mermaid! a mermaid!" he breathes in affright;
> Yet through him thrills quick a mysterious delight.
> –The Duchess of Kent, *The New Monthly Belle Assemblee* (1848)

Two-tailed water nymphs are steeped in legend. "Half-human, half-monstrous, and a fairy tale creation associated with art and magic,"[1] mermaids with two fishy extremities have illustrated alchemical treatises, been carved into fertility charms in Italy, and proudly exhibited on the family crests of France, Germany, and England. (Heraldic tradition refers to these creatures as *Melusine*, "the quintessential medieval fatal attraction."[2]) In the superstition and mythology of the Shetland Islands, the "haff-fish" or *selkie* is a fallen spirit, and misfortune is said to follow the wretched destroyer of one of these creatures.[3] In Greek legend, mermaids were known as *sirens*, their beguiling voices luring sailors to their doom, though "in Roman art they were benign beings who

A water nymph wearing a shell necklace overlooks the stairway to the estuary.

---

1 Rachel Hadas, *Form, Cycle, Infinity* (1985)
2 Donald Maddox and Sara Sturm-Maddox, *Melusine of Lusignan* (1996)
3 John Vinycomb, *Fictitious & Symbolic Creatures in Art* (1906)

An ironwork two-tailed mermaid sits above the archway of Bridge House.

consoled the departed with their sweet song."[4] Elsewhere, mermaids have been revered as goddesses. "A Semetic mermaid moon-goddess, called Atargatis among the Syrians and Derceto among the Philistines, was widely worshiped."[5]

The enchanting song of two-tailed mermaids fills every corner of Portmeirion, as the exotic creatures figure into a great many ironwork panels. Clough salvaged around thirty panels from the Seaman's Home in Liverpool. How many mermaids can you spot? Note that they are variously painted blue, white, cream, and combinations thereof.

A stone mermaid greets visitors to the Shell Grotto. One tail or two?

---

4 Anthony Weir and James Jerman, *Images of Lust: Sexual Carvings on Medieval Churches* (1993)
5 Malcolm South, *Mythical and Fabulous Creatures* (1987)

Even the sheet metal *trompe l'oeil* mermaid near the tollgate is two-tailed, though her tails rest side-by-side instead of spread apart. The plaque on the front wall of the Government House and the carving on the archway linking the Round House to Prior's Lodging likewise depict two-tailed mermaids. Neptune Cottage's signature plaque depicts a two-tailed triton, and statue of a young triton with two tails overlooks the fish pond outside Mermaid Cottage.

A two-tailed mermaid crest high above the archway of Bridge House.

In the ironwork panels, each bare-breasted mermaid wields two criss-crossed ship anchors which intersect a double-headed trident. The

Above the Round House archway, a two-tailed mermaid is carved into a shell carried by two sea horses.

twinning of anchors, tridents, and tails speaks to the creature's dual nature: divine and demonic, consoling and slaughtering, buoying and sinking. The mermaid's Mona Lisa smile perfectly captures her ambiguous character. Ultimately, she represents the dark side of the Greek love goddess Aphrodite, "her two thrashing tails symbolizing the birth and the death of Her affections," reminding us of how instinctive energy "comes from a deep, unconscious part of ourselves."[6]

A two-tailed merman guards the entrance to Neptune Cottage.

---

6 Shekhinah Mountainwater, *Ariadne's Thread* (1991)

Scavenger Hunt: The Elusive Unicorn

The "Fairest Jewel" in Mythology

In the great Welsh myth *Mabinogion*, a stag with a single, spear-length horn in its forehead is the "fairest jewel" in the dominion of the great faery queen Rhiannon. The unicorn, described as being swift as a bird, is notorious for drinking from ponds and exposing the fish to the fatal rays of the sun. Unicorn watchers will want to spend time around fish ponds in the Portmeirion woodlands. The author will gratefully appreciate details of any unicorn sightings.

The elusive unicorn makes three artistic appearances in Portmeirion. Can you find them? (Answers on the following page.)

Answers to the scavenger hunt for the elusive unicorn. Previous page, a unicorn ornament at the back of Unicorn Cottage (not accessible by day visitors). Its twin adorns the front of Unicorn Cottage. Above, a unicorn statue sits above the archway to Unicorn Cottage.

Scavenger Hunt: Grotesqueries

Comic Distortions

It's only natural that a preposterous village would offer asylum to grotesque figures. However, most of the unsightly faces at Portmeirion are hiding in the shadows. Can you find them? (Answers on the next page.)

Answers to the scavenger hunt for grotesqueries. Previous page, a severely damaged ornament inside the Bristol Colonnade. Above, a detail of one of the twin wooden columns inside the Gothic Pavilion. Both wooden columns are, as of this writing, significantly damaged. Next page, the top of the Gothic Pavilion features many grotesque faces.

Scavenger Hunt: Mother and Cherub Reunion

Waifs and Strays

Taliesin, the great bard of Welsh mythology, was a foundling. The tales of the *Mabinogion* relate that Taliesin's mother, the goddess Ceridwen, abandoned her baby, throwing him to sea in a leather bag. The baby floated for nine days and nights before being caught by Elffin, a fisherman. Elffin marveled at the infant's beauty and named him Taliesin, meaning "radiant brow."

Portmeirion is a veritable orphanage—a city of lost cherubim. The strays are easy to spot, from the two little angels atop the Gloriette, to the cherub supporting the sun dial near the Bristol Colonnade, to the young triton overlooking the fish pond next to Mermaid Cottage, to the cherub situated in the magnificent cliff beneath Chantry Cottage, to the Dionysian angels carved into the rendezvous seat in the middle of Salutation carpark, to the statue of the girl cradling a puppy in an alcove of the Campanile (not visible to day visitors), to the two cherubs in a plaque high above the Bridge House archway.

But can you find two examples of little ones reunited with their mothers? (Answers on the next page.)

Answers to the scavenger hunt for mothers and cherubim. At the back of Mermaid Cottage (above), a statue representing Charity carries one babe and leads another by the hand. Next page, an archway leading to the Dome Flat depicts a haloed Madonna hugging a haloed child (not accessible by day visitors).

Scavenger Hunt: Bells and Whistles

Ringing Silence

In Welsh mythology, King Arthur and the warriors of the Island of the Mighty sleep under a great bronze bell the size of a beehive, ready to be awakened if Wales falls into danger.[1] The many bells throughout Portmeirion are all out of reach, as if reserved for emergencies. If any bell ever makes a sound, it will merely be the wind whistling through the hollows. Whatever practical purpose the bells once had, today they serve as silent ornaments.

How many bells can you find throughout the village? (Answers on the next page.)

---

1   Gwynn Jones, *Tales From Wales* (2001)

Answers to the scavenger hunt for bells. Previous page, the bell at Toll House, once used to summon the gatekeeper. Above, a phoenix bell at the Portmeirion Hotel. More answers follow.

Above, one of two bells on the Chinese ironwork arch next to the Playhouse.

Above, a bell at Angel Cottage (top) and above the stairs to Lady's Lodge (bottom). Next page, the bells of the Campanile, as seen from the estuary side (not accessible by day visitors).

Scavenger Hunt: Paragons of Virtue

> My dear little Welsh angel—you shall have it all complete . . . all the poetic mind could desire.
> —Dion Boucicault, *The Phantom: A Drama, in Two Acts* (1857)

On a Wing and a Prayer

Cherubs aside, Portmeirion is a haven for a variety of celestial beings. These winged angels bespeak aspirations and adoration, guidance and guardianship, prophecy and purity.

How many divine messengers can you find? (Answers on the next page.)

Answers to the scavenger hunt for angels. Previous page, an angel relief on the front of Angel Cottage. Above, two angels on the archway leading to Chantry Row (not accessible by day visitors). More answers follow.

Above, one of several angels on the side of Ship Shop (top) and two mermaid-like angels above the door to Round House (below).

Above, an angel painting on the side of Arches Cottage. Next page, an angel relief on the side of Toll House.

Above, the angel on the side of Angel Cottage.

Portmeirion as a Sailor's Knot*

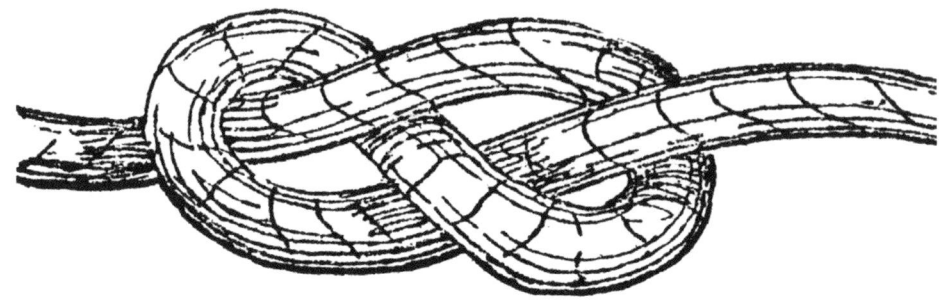

String Theory

According to the String Theory of physics, the universe is held together by elastic bands. Portmeirion, with its twisting pathways, is like a knot in the strings of this world. Imagine a string as a beaded necklace. When we lose something, like an old building, the necklace gets smaller, and sometimes the entire strand of beads falls away. In other words, when a single building topples, it carries with it a host of memories, history, and significance. One loss can trigger a chain reaction. Portmeirion ties a knot, so that the entire string of beads doesn't fall apart.

By reassembling lost architecture, Portmeirion serves as a makeshift way station—a stopgap measure demonstrating perseverance. This way station reestablishes connections, like a switch board. It maintains integrity, like cement. It keeps things from getting lost, like an anchor. As repository of memories, Portmeirion keeps people from forgetting old stories even as it spins new ones.

Portmeirion invites us to dance along its twisting strands and to marvel at all the beauties held together in perfect balance. Like a burlap canvas, it stretches the fabric of space/time and encourages us to fabricate. If anything, Portmeirion continually invites metaphor, like a word applied to an object to which it is not literally applicable.

* Inspired by Haruki Murakami's *Dance Dance Dance* (1994).

Woodland Trail Maps

The trees have eyes in the Portmeirion woodlands.

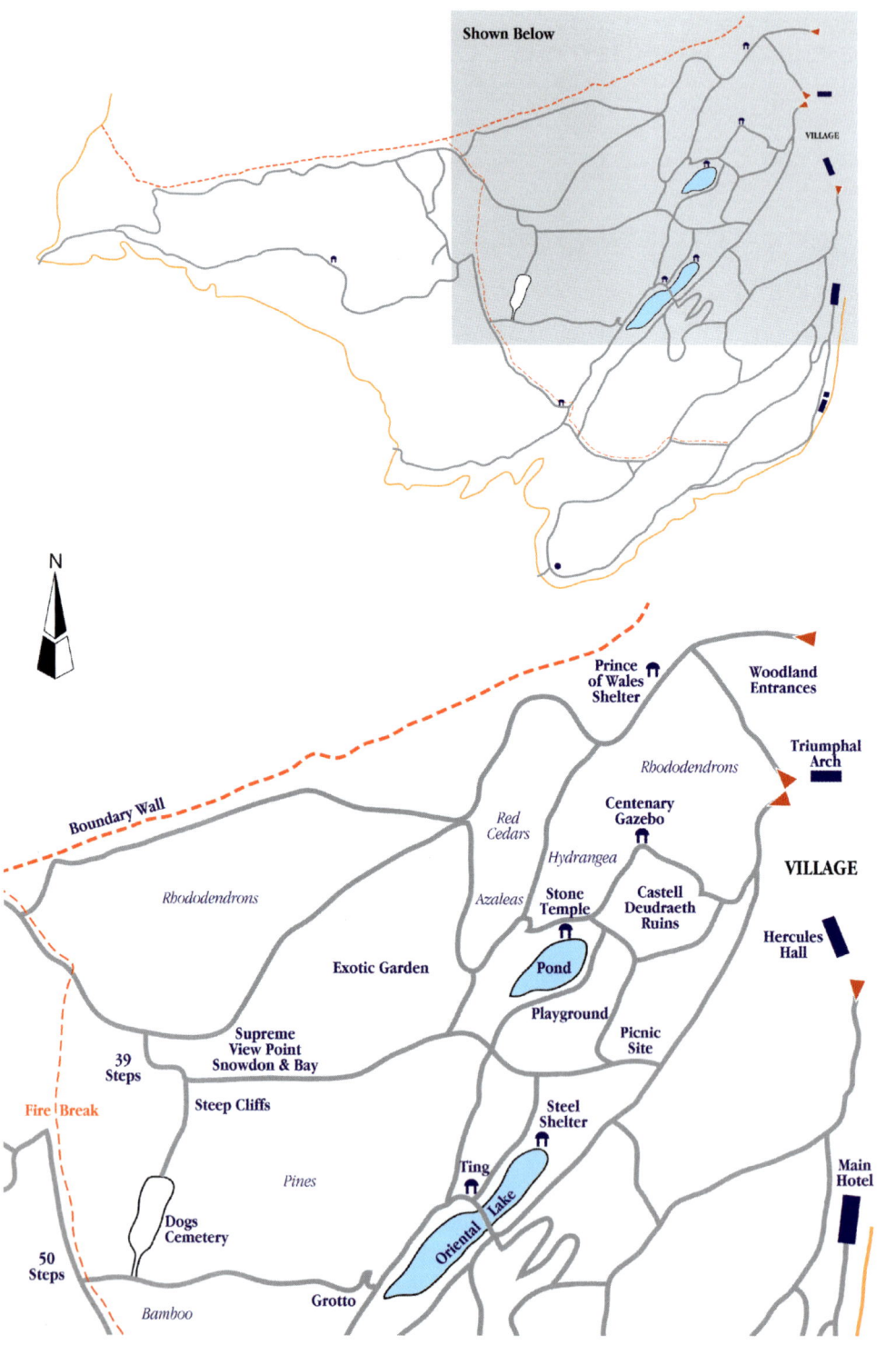

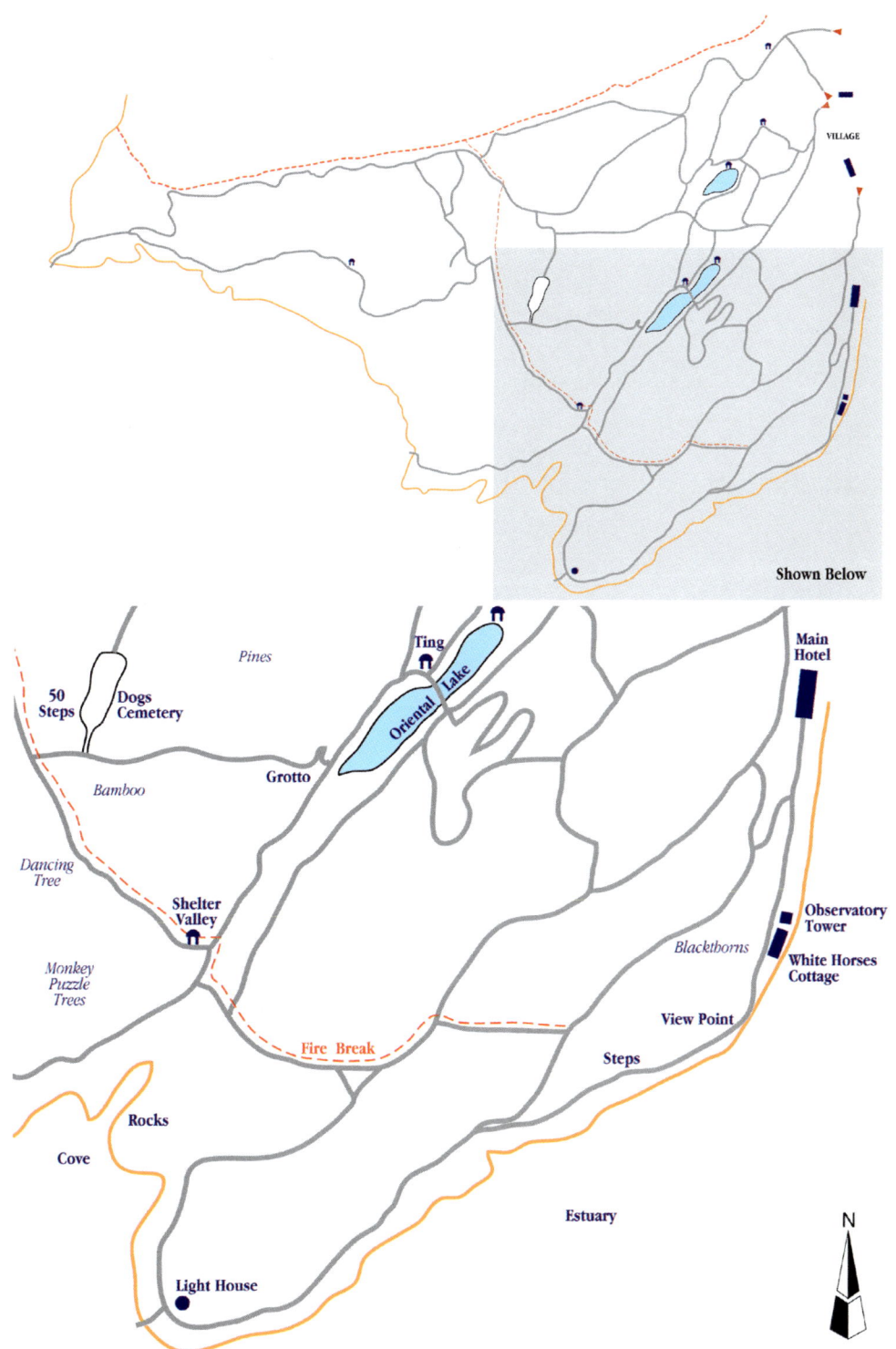

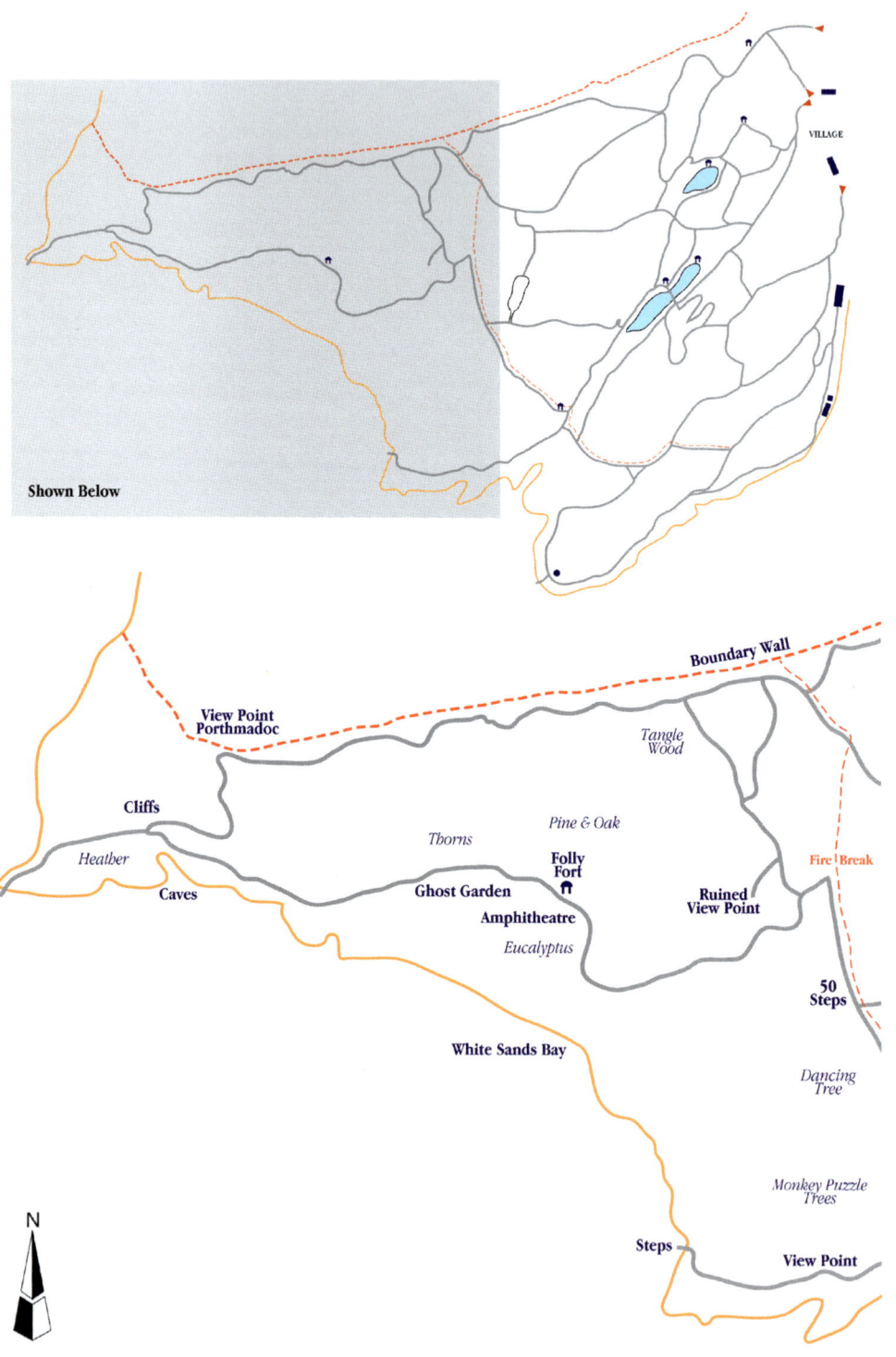

Printed in Great Britain
by Amazon